CHASIDISM

CHASIDISM

ITS DEVELOPMENT, THEOLOGY, AND PRACTICE

NOSON GURARY

JASON ARONSON INC.
Northvale, New Jersey
Jerusalem

This book was set in 11 pt. Berkeley Book by Alabama Book Composition of Deatsville, Alabama, and printed and bound by Book-mart Press of North Bergen, New Jersey.

Library of Congress Cataloging-in-Publication Data

Gurary, Natan (Guraryeh)
    Chasidism : its development, theology, and practice / Noson Gurary.
        p.   cm.
    Includes index.
    ISBN 0–7657–5960–8 (alk. paper)
    1. Hasidism.   I. Title.
BM198.2.G87   1997
296.8′332—DC20   96-41908

Manufactured in the United States of America. Jason Aronson Inc. offers books and cassettes. For information and catalog write to Jason Aronson Inc., 230 Livingston Street, Northvale, New Jersey 07647.

CONTENTS

INTRODUCTION

Jewish mysticism teaches that the purpose of the soul's descent to earth is to reveal the harmony that is inherent in the created world, beginning with the "small world," namely, man—a creature of *nigleh* ["revealed aspects"] and *nistar* ["hidden aspects"], of a body and a soul. Inner personal peace and harmony can be achieved only through the supremacy of the soul over the body, since in the nature and scheme of things, the body can be made to submit to the soul—willingly, and in the case of the true mystic, even eagerly—but not vice versa.

Jewish mysticism helps to realize the said purpose of the soul by teaching it how to recognize the spirituality of matter, and that in every physical thing, even in the inanimate, there is a "soul," which is the creative force that has created it—a being out of nonbeing—and which continuously keeps it from reverting back to its former state of non-existence. It is this "spark" of Godliness that is the true essence and reality of all things, and this spark is released and revealed when physical matter is used for a sublime purpose or deed in accordance with the Will of the Creator—as for example, in the performance of a commandment (*mitzvah*).

[One of the axioms of Chasidic thought is that] in the final analysis, God can be "comprehended" better by action (the performance of the *mitzvahs*) than by meditation, which is one of the cardinal differences between Jewish and non-Jewish mysticism.[1]

The above description of Jewish mysticism serves as the guideline to this study of the development, theology, and practices of the school of Chasidism, founded by the Ba'al Shem Tov in the eighteenth century. It is clear that the mystical theology of Chasidism is very different from other forms of mysticism—both Eastern and Western. In this sense, chasidic mysticism might be said to be revolutionary. How this is so will become clear in this work.

The first part of this study is a general survey of the ethos of Chasidism. Chasidism's self-perception regarding the movement's essence and purpose, and its creative contribution to Jewish thought, as compared with the schools of *Kabbalah, Chakira, and Mussar*, will also be examined. These preliminary subjects will help us to understand the major aim of this study—which is to clarify some of the most important axioms of chasidic mystical theology. We will begin with the chasidic view of the purpose of creation and the mission of man in this world. This will be followed by a general overview of the highly esoteric Lurianic doctrine of *tzimtzum*, as explained by various schools of thought. Thus, we will come to an understanding of the Oneness of the Creator and the ultimate spirituality of matter. We will see how this is reflected in the Ba'al Shem Tov's explanation of Divine Providence, in the chasidic understanding of the nature of truth, and in the purpose and function of Torah—which is to reveal the purpose of creation and the mission of man, the Oneness of the Creator and the ultimate spirituality of matter.

---

1. From a letter by the seventh Lubavitcher Rebbe, Rabbi M. M. Schneerson, written to the organizers of the International Seminar on Jewish Mysticism (held in London, 1981).

Finally, we will show that the existential and cosmological views maintained by Chasidism do not contradict human experience or the religious values of normative Judaism as expressed in the *Halachic* codes. On the contrary, Chasidism demands their ultimate synthesis and actualization in daily life.

1
THE CHASIDIC ETHOS

1

THE ORIGINS OF CHASIDISM, THE BA'AL SHEM TOV, AND ACHIYA HASHILONI

This introductory section will not attempt to give a comprehensive socio-historical analysis of the rise and development of Chasidism, for that subject has already been treated in a wide range of books and papers. Rather, we will make a number of observations and clarifications (some historical and some philosophical) that are important for the proper understanding of Chasidism in general and of the intellectually oriented *Chabad* school in particular. The latter is an important branch of Chasidism and some of its ideas deserve special attention. This will be followed by a delineation of the essence of Chasidism and its creative contribution to Jewish thought and practice. Finally, we will examine the reasons for the advent of the *Chabad* school,

3

as found in the teachings and writings of the seventh Rebbe of
Chabad, Rabbi M. M. Schneerson.

The inception of Chasidism is described in the following letter[1]
from its founder, Rabbi Israel, best known as the Ba'al Shem Tov
(1698–1760),[2] to his brother-in-law, who lived in Israel at the
time. It describes his mystical experience, which led to the
establishment of Chasidism and which serves as its raison d'etre:[3]

> On *Rosh Hashanah* [the Jewish New Year's day] of the year 5507
> [1746], I brought about an ascent of soul using Holy Names,[4] as
> you are familiar with, and I saw wondrous things which I had never
> seen since the day I attained knowledge. What I saw
> and learned there I cannot recount, nor speak about even face-
> to-face. . . . I also saw a number of souls, of the living and of the
> dead, some known to me, and some unknown to me . . . and all of
> them, as one, beseeched me incessantly, "Ascend with us, and be our
> aid and support. . . ." I said that I would ascend with them, but I

---

1. *Keter Shem Tov* (Kehot, 1973) chap. 1. This letter was first printed
in 1781 by R. Yaakov Yosef of Polonnoye, one of the chief disciples of the
Ba'al Shem Tov. See N. Loewenthal, *Communicating the Infinite* (University of Chicago Press, 1990), p. 6ff, for an enlightening discussion of this
letter in the context of *Merkavah* mysticism.

2. This is the date of his birth according to Hasidic and *Chabad*
tradition. See C. Glitzenshtein, R. Israel Ba'al Shem Tov, pp. 12, 17. S.
Horodetzky, *Hasidism v'haHasidim*, sect. 1, p. 1, and S. Dubnow, *Toldot
HaHasidism*, p. 42, maintain that he was born in 1700.

3. This letter is generally regarded as authentic even by the most
skeptical of scholars. See S. Dubnow, *History of Hasidism*, p. 60; G.
Scholem, *The Messianic Idea in Judaism*, p. 182. Regarding the impor-
tance of this letter in the early generations of Hasidism, see Horodetzky,
Ha-Hasidism v'ha-Hasidim, vol. 1 (1928), p. 56; B. Z. Dinur, *B'mifneh
HaDorot* (1972), p. 183, n. 8. Other scholars, such as Scholem and
Tishby, have also stressed the importance of this letter.

4. In the original—*hashba'at aliyat ha-neshamah*. See *Eitz Chaim*,
sha'ar 39, chap. 4.

asked my teacher and master to accompany me, because of the great
danger in going further and ascending to the upper worlds. . . . I
rose from level to level until I entered the Chamber of the Messiah,[5]
where he learns Torah[6] with all the Sages of the *Mishnah*, with the
righteous, and also with the Seven Shepherds.[7] . . . I asked the
Messiah himself, "When will you come?"[8] He replied, "Through this
you will know—when your teachings will become known and will
be revealed in the world, and your wellsprings shall burst forth,
[bringing] to the outside that which I have taught you, and you have
comprehended, so that they,[9] too, will be able to make unifications
and ascents [of soul] just like you.[10] Then all of the evil *kelipot*[11] will
cease to be, and it will be the era of goodwill and salvation." I was
shocked at this and had great anguish at the extraordinary length of
time—when could this possibly be? However, from what I learned
while I was there—three *segulot*[12] and three Holy Names, which are
easy to learn and explain—I was [somewhat] mollified. I thought
that perhaps by this means those of spiritual stature similar to mine[13]

---

5. See *Eitz Chaim*, sha'ar 46.

6. The generic term for the Written Law (including the Pentateuch,
the Prophetic writings, etc.) and the Oral Law (including *Mishnah,*
Talmud, Midrash, Midrash Halachah, and later works).

7. From the verse in *Michah* 5:4. They are: "David in the middle;
Adam, Seth, and Methuselah to his right; Abraham, Jacob, and Moses to
his left" (*Sukkah* 52b; *Shir HaShirim Rabbah* 8:11).

8. Cf. *Sanhedrin* 98a, which discusses a similar exchange between R.
Yehoshua ben Levi and the Messiah.

9. Those who are in the category of "outside," signifying ordinary
people who do not possess lofty souls and have not purified themselves,
as will be explained in chapter 2.

10. This will be explained at length later.

11. "Husks" or "shells"—a mystical term for the forces of evil that
conceal the divine spark contained within all of creation.

12. *Segulot* (singular, *segulah*) could be rendered as "especially
effective or beneficial means or techniques." It generally denotes
something possessing effective mystical power.

13. Literally, "men of my age."

will be able to attain a level and aspect like mine. That is, because they will be able to ascend [on high], they will learn and comprehend just as I [learned and comprehended]. But permission was not granted during my entire life for me to reveal this. . . .

It will be noted by anyone familiar with chasidic teachings that three of the cardinal principles emphasized throughout the Ba'al Shem Tov's teachings, and those of his disciples, are to be found in this letter: Love of one's fellow Jew, even one whose heart has strayed from the path of truth and must be returned to its Father in Heaven; spreading forth the wellsprings of knowledge contained in the esoteric wisdom of the Torah; and preparing oneself and the world for the advent of the Messiah.[14]

Several important questions arise concerning this letter: Who is the personage to whom the Ba'al Shem Tov refers as "my teacher and master?" What are these three *segulot* and three Holy Names? If permission was not granted to the Ba'al Shem Tov during his life to reveal these *segulot* and Holy Names, when were they transmitted, if at all, and to whom?

Chasidic tradition[15] explains that the teacher and master of the

---

14. *Likkutei Sichot*, vol. 2, p. 512, n. 62. See also the discourse of *Simchat Torah* 5690, delivered by Rabbi Joseph I. Schneerson in 1930.

15. *Toldot Ya'akov Yosef, Balak*; *Sefer HaSichot* 5700, p. 159; *Likkutei Sichot*, vol. 2, p. 512, n. 62. *Sefer HaSichot* cites a letter from the Ba'al Shem Tov himself to this effect, printed in *Hatamim*, vol. 4, p. 18. The letter is from the Herson Genizah, about which there is much controversy. Many scholars reject its authenticity, but there is no doubt that *Chabad* sources openly accept the Genizah as authentic, and the contents of the letters as genuine, although the letters themselves are acknowledged as copies and not as the originals. The entire matter is discussed from the *Chabad* point of view by the Lubavitcher Rebbe, Rabbi M. M. Schneerson, in a long article at the end of *Igrot Kodesh Admor HaZaken, Admor HaEmtza'i, Admor HaTzemach Tzedek* (Kehot, 1980), pp. 469–487.

Ba'al Shem Tov was the Prophet Achiya HaShiloni,[16] whose soul was first revealed to the Ba'al Shem Tov on his twenty-sixth birthday.[17] The theme of guidance by the soul of a prophet or saintly person from former times is not new in kabbalistic thought. It has been discussed at length by R. Chaim Vital, the chief disciple of R. Yitzchak Luria, the famous kabbalist of Safed, Israel, best known as the *Arizal* (1534–1572). R. Chaim Vital was an important Kabbalist in his own right, and was a prolific writer. In *Sha'arei Kedushah*[18] he describes various forms of Divine Inspiration:[19]

> One who is worthy can have Divine Inspiration in one of the following ways: (1) By drawing down upon his soul a supernal light from the highest root of his soul,[20] which becomes revealed to him. This is pure Divine Inspiration. (2) Through occupying himself with Torah study or fulfilling a commandment (*mitzvah*).[21] Our Sages taught,[22] "When a person fulfills a *mitzvah*, he acquires a [heavenly] advocate for himself." That is, an angel is actually assigned [to him] but only on condition that he fulfills [the *mitzvah*] consistently, according to the law, and with great

---

16. Mentioned in 1 Kings 11:29, 30; 12:15; 14:2, 4, et al., and in *Talmud Yerushalmi, Berachot* 9:2; *Bereishit Rabbah* 35:2; *Pesikta d'Rav Kahana*, s.v., in connection with Rabbi Shimon bar Yochai, author of the *Zohar* (according to traditional Jewish sources. This is certainly the *Chabad* view).

17. *Sefer HaSichot* 5700, p. 159.

18. Pt. 3, *sha'ar* 7.

19. *Ruach HaKodesh*, in the original.

20. See below, section 2, chap. 2, where we discuss the five levels, or roots, of the soul.

21. Obviously, this does not mean that he neglects any of the other commandments. R. Chaim Vital explains in pt. 3, *sha'ar* 3, 4, that proper fulfillment of all the commandments is a prerequisite to the acquisition of *Ruach HaKodesh*.

22. *Avot* 4:13.

concentration.[23] Then the angel will reveal itself to him. This is the meaning of those angels called *maggidim*, which are mentioned in various writings.[24] However, if the commandment is not observed in [strict] accordance with the law, the *maggid* will be an admixture of good and evil, truth and falsehood. (3) As a result of a person's great piety, Elijah [the Prophet] will reveal himself to the person. The greater one's piety, the greater will be one's enlightenment. (4) The greatest of all [forms of Divine Inspiration] is when a person is worthy of the revelation of the soul of a saintly person (*tzaddik*) from an earlier era who has since passed away. This *tzaddik* may be from among those who have the same soul-root as his. Alternatively, [the soul of the *tzaddik*] may be not be from this category, but [his soul becomes revealed to the person] because he fulfilled a commandment perfectly, just as he [the *tzaddik*] had done. Those who are worthy of this superior level gain the most wondrous knowledge and the secrets of the Torah. However, all of this is commensurate with a person's deeds. (5) The lowest aspect of them all is when he sees the future in his dreams, and [he gains] knowledge akin to Divine Inspiration. . . .

Following the above analysis, we could postulate that the Ba'al Shem Tov had acquired the highest form of Divine Inspiration — the soul of a *tzaddik* from an earlier era (in this case, the soul of Achiya HaShiloni) became revealed to him (as described in No. 4 above).[25]

Who was Achiya HaShiloni, and what was his connection to the Ba'al Shem Tov and the esoteric teachings of the Torah? We have very little direct information in this regard, but some light is

---

23. *Kavvanah* in the original; sometimes translated as "intention."

24. The most famous of these is the *maggid* of R. Yosef Caro, the author of the *Shulchan Aruch* and a contemporary of the *Arizal*. In his book entitled *Maggid Mesharim*, he describes at length his daily encounters with his *maggid*, and many of the teachings that the *maggid* communicated to him.

25. See *Tanya*, end of chap. 14.

shed on the subject by ancient midrashic sources:[26] Several midrashic sources cite the statement of R. Shimon bar Yochai, the master of the inner dimensions of the Torah, that he could exempt the entire world from harsh judgments until the advent of the messianic era if Achiya HaShiloni joined him.[27] Rabbi Menachem M. Schneerson, the seventh Lubavitcher Rebbe, suggests that this could be explained according to a kabbalistic source[28] that states that R. Shimon Bar Yochai was, in fact, an incarnation of Achiya HaShiloni. R. Shimon bar Yochai states explicitly in the *Zohar*[29] that the Jewish people will be redeemed from the exile "in a compassionate manner" through tasting the esoteric teachings of the *Zohar*. According to the Ba'al Shem Tov's letter cited above, he was given the mission of revealing these esoteric teachings to the world at large in order to prepare the way for the advent of the Messiah. It is therefore fitting that he should have the *ibbur neshamah* (the "impregnation" of soul) of Achiya HaShiloni.

Regarding Achiya HaShiloni, one of the forty-eight Hebrew Prophets, Maimonides[30] writes that,

Achiya HaShiloni received [the Tradition] from Moses, and was one of those who left Egypt [in the Exodus of the Israelites]. Subsequently, he was a member of the Rabbinical Court of King David. He was also the master of Elijah the Prophet.[31] R. Ya'akov Yosef of Polonnoye, one of the earliest and closest disciples of the Ba'al Shem Tov, cites Maimonides and adds that Achiya HaShiloni

---

26. See *Likkutei Sichot*, vol. 2, p. 512, n. 62.

27. This is according to the version found in *Talmud Yerushalmi*, *Berachot*, 9:2; *Bereshit Rabbah* 35:2; *Pesikta d'Rav Kahana*, s.v.

28. End of R. Yitzchak Luria's *Sefer HaGilgulim*.

29. Vol. 3, p. 124b.

30. *Code*, Introduction.

31. See also *Toledot Ya'akov Yosef*, *Balak*. Ra'avad, a contemporary of Maimonides, disagrees that Achiya was the master of Elijah. He argues that Achiya was Elijah's **disciple**.

was also "the master of my teacher, [the Ba'al Shem Tov]." From this, it appears that Achiya's role as the mentor of the Ba'al Shem Tov is connected to his role as the master of Elijah the Prophet, Rabbi Schneerson continues. It is Elijah's duty to prepare the world for the advent of the Messiah, by bringing back those who have strayed afar, as stated in the verse, "I am sending you Elijah the Prophet prior to the Great Day [of the advent of the Messiah] and he will return the hearts . . ."[32]

Thus the connection between Achiya HaShiloni and the Ba'al Shem Tov is bound up with preparing the world for the messianic era.

What were the three *segulot* and the three Holy Names which were given to the Ba'al Shem Tov and that he was not granted permission to divulge? There is very little, if any, concrete historical evidence that will allow us to state categorically what they were. Nevertheless, there are some interesting speculations in this regard.

Concerning the Holy Names given to the Ba'al Shem Tov, there is an oral tradition maintained by *Chabad chasidim*[33] that two of the Holy Names are those pertaining to *yichuda ila'ah* (the upper unity, in which all of creation is nullified in the all-encompassing Being of God); and *yichuda tata'ah* (the lower unity, in which Godliness permeates all of creation, including spatial and temporal dimensions). Rabbi Shneur Zalman of Liadi states[34] that the Name signifying *yichuda ila'ah* is formed "by the intertwining

---

32. Malachi 3:23. See the *Mishnah* at the conclusion of the tract *Eduyot*, and other places.

33. Confirmed by R. Y. Mondshein, of the Manuscript Division of the Hebrew University of Jerusalem's library, in a conversation with this author.

34. *Tanya, Sha'ar HaYichud v'haEmunah*, chap. 7, p. 82a.

of the [letters of the] Name *Adnut*[35] within the letters of the Tetragrammaton,"[36] while the Name signifying *yichuda tata'ah* is formed "by the intertwining of the [letters of the] the Tetragrammaton within the letters of the Name *Adnut*." He explains further:

> The life-force of space, and likewise of time, and their coming into being *ex nihilo*,[37] and their existence, as long as they continue to exist, is from the attribute of His *malchut*[38] . . . and the Name of *Adnut* . . . Now, since the attribute of His *malchut* . . . is united with His Essence and Being in an absolute union[39] . . . therefore space and time are also completely nullified in relation to his Essence and Being, may He be blessed, just as the light of the sun is nullified in the sun.
>
> And this is the [meaning of] the intertwining of the [letters of the] Name *Adnut* within the [letters of the] Tetragrammaton. The Tetragrammaton indicates that He transcends time, for "He was, He is, and He will be at the same instant," as is explained [in *Ra'ya Mehemna* on the portion of *Pinchas*].[40] Likewise, He transcends space, for He continually creates all the dimensions of space everywhere, from highest to lowest and in all four directions.

The foregoing is an explanation of *yichuda ila'ah*, in which all of existence is nullified in the all-encompassing Being of God. What

---

35. *A-d-o-n-a-i*, signifying "rulership" or "mastery." This name therefore pertains to creation, since "there is no king without a people" (*Emek HaMelech*).

36. "The Ineffable Name," signifying the infinite transcendence of God.

37. Cf. Maimonides, *Guide for the Perplexed* 2, 13; R. Menachem Mendel of Lubavitch (*Tzemach Tzedek*) *Derech Mitzvotecha* (Brooklyn: Kehot, 1953), pp. 113–114.

38. "Royalty, dominion." This refers to the attribute from whence creation derives, as explained in the text.

39. As he explains in *Sha'ar HaYichud v'haEmunah*, chap. 8.

40. Zohar, Vol. 3, p. 257b.

follows is the explanation of *yichuda tata'ah*, in which Godliness permeates all of creation, including spatial and temporal dimensions:

> Now, although He transcends both space and time, nevertheless, He is also found below in space and time. That is, He unites with His attribute of *malchut* from which space and time are derived and come into existence. This is *yichuda tata'ah*, [the intertwining of the] Tetragrammaton within (the letters of the Name) *Adnut*. That is, His Essence and Being . . . which is called by the Name of *Ein Sof* ("Infinite"), completely fills the whole earth temporally and spatially.

Since the Ba'al Shem Tov states explicitly in the letter cited above that he was forbidden to reveal the secrets that he had been given, how was his message transmitted? One possibility is that he incorporated the *segulot* and the Holy Names into his lessons and private oral communications to his disciples, as well as into the directives he gave them concerning their daily observance of Torah, *mitzvot*, and prayer. In this regard, an account of the various means of transmission of the "theurgic tradition"—that is, the transmission of mystical experience and power—has been given by other writers.[41]

A second possibility is that the Ba'al Shem Tov communicated his teachings to his disciples, and perhaps to their disciples as well, after his passing (". . . permission was not given during my entire life for me to reveal this"), in much the same way that he himself had received the teachings from his own mentor, Achiya HaShiloni, as described above.

Regarding the granting of permission to communicate the teachings (if not the direct communication of the teachings themselves), *Chabad* tradition relates the following story, which

---

41. See Loewenthal, *Communicating the Infinite*, particularly pp. 6ff, 43–44.

took place during Rabbi Shneur Zalman's incarceration in a Russian prison as a result of the false accusations leveled against him by the opponents of Chasidism, the *mitnagdim*:

> Before he went on trial, his master, the Maggid of Mezritch, and the Ba'al Shem Tov came from the World of Truth to visit him. Rabbi Shneur Zalman asked them why he had been falsely accused and imprisoned, and what was required of him in the circumstances. They answered that the [heavenly] accusation against him was due to the extent that he had revealed and publicized the esoteric teachings. Rabbi Shneur Zalman then asked the Maggid of Mezritch and the Ba'al Shem Tov if he should stop doing so when he would be released. But they replied that he should not stop. Since he had started, he should not cease—on the contrary, after his release he should continue in even greater measure [this, in fact, took place, as is evident[42] from Rabbi Shneur Zalman's writings before and after his imprisonment.][43] Rabbi Shneur Zalman asked them for their help in this regard, which was duly given, along with their blessings.[44]

Hillman, the chronicler of the story, adds that there are more details to tell in this regard, but that a historical account of the first three generations of *Chabad* leaders is not the proper forum.

It is clear that Rabbi Shneur Zalman took this visitation seriously and viewed his subsequent acquittal as a heavenly vindication and an endorsement of his path. Furthermore, we see from a later conversation he had with a friend and colleague, R. Levi Yitzchak of Berditchev, that he believed that not only had he been given permission to reveal and disseminate the teachings of

---

42. See also Loewenthal, *Communicating the Infinite*, p. 71ff. This matter will be discussed further on in our introduction.

43. Known in *Chabad* tradition as "before or after Petersburg." See *Torat Shalom* (Kehot, 1983), p. 112ff. See, further, in chap. 2.

44. The story appears in Hillman, *Beit Rebbe*, pt. 1, chap. 16, n. 2. An account of the entire episode can be found in *Beit Rebbe*, chaps. 14–19.

the Ba'al Shem Tov, he had actually been given the explicit mission of doing so:

> At the wedding of their grandchildren in Zhlobin, R. Levi Yitzchak questioned the authority given to Rabbi Shneur Zalman to reveal the secrets of the Torah to the extent that he did, particularly in view of the fact that the Ba'al Shem Tov had cautioned his own grandson, R. Aharon Tutoiever of Kitov, that "It is the glory of God to conceal a thing" (Proverbs 25:2), indicating that esoteric matters should remain hidden. Rabbi Shneur Zalman replied that the Ba'al Shem Tov had instructed him differently. "When did you see the Ba'al Shem Tov?" asked R. Levi Yitzchak. (Rabbi Shneur Zalman never met the Ba'al Shem Tov face-to-face, although the latter passed away when Rabbi Shneur Zalman was already fifteen years old. According to *Chabad* tradition, the Ba'al Shem Tov deliberately avoided meeting with the young Rabbi Shneur Zalman, because the latter "belonged to the Maggid.").[45] Rabbi Shneur Zalman replied, "When I was in prison in Petersburg." R. Levi Yitzchak then asked, "While you were awake, or in a dream?" "While I was awake," he answered, and this ended the conversation.[46]

It is important to note that R. Levi Yitzchak did not argue with Rabbi Shneur Zalman as to the authenticity of his experience or as to the validity of the mission he had received. This certainly indicates that R. Levi Yitzchak accepted Rabbi Shneur Zalman's authority to continue disseminating the secrets of Torah in the way that he had been doing.

In conclusion, it is clear that the Ba'al Shem Tov regarded the mystical experience in which he conversed with the Messiah as absolutely valid and that he was certain that he had been given the mission of preparing the world for the advent of the Messiah

---

45. C. Glitzenshtein, *Sefer HaToldot, Admor HaZaken.*

46. R. Raphael Kahan, *Shemu'ot v'Sippurim*, vol. 3. (Brooklyn, 1990), p. 158; R. Y. Chitrik, *Reshimat Devarim*, vol. 3, (Brooklyn, 1989), p. 95.

by revealing and disseminating the teachings with which he had been entrusted. So, too, Rabbi Shneur Zalman regarded his communication with the Ba'al Shem Tov as absolutely valid; the mission to prepare the world for the advent of the Messiah by disseminating the teachings given to the Ba'al Shem Tov had now devolved upon him.

2

THE ADVENT OF THE CHABAD SCHOOL

The Ba'al Shem Tov began disseminating his teachings on a scale probably unprecedented in the history of Jewish mysticism. He propagated the ideas and ideals of the inner dimensions of Torah in a way that could be absorbed by all, even the unlearned. He spent much of his time traveling through the towns and villages populated by simple Jews, where he would address his audiences with apparently simple stories, or with perceptive comments on the events described in the Torah. He taught that every Jew is capable of serving God with love and reverence, even if he lacked scholarship. Simple folk, through sincere recitation of prayers and psalms (though ignorant of the meaning of the words) and through love of their fellow Jew, are able to achieve inner closeness to God—for the overriding consideration is the actual deed and sincere worship. These matters were easily understood by the simple folk at whom they were directed and were sufficient to inflame their souls with love for God, His people, and His Torah. Thenceforth, the ordinary person could return to his mundane tasks and often poverty-stricken life with renewed vigor and enthusiasm. The Ba'al Shem Tov's words, however, were invariably based on, and alluded to, profound insights of the mystical depths of the Torah. His scholarly disciples, who often accompanied him on these journeys, were able to understand the inner essence of his teachings, despite their apparently simple form, and would meditate deeply upon them, deriving inspiration and new understanding of the depths of the Torah.

The following generation, under the leadership of R. Dov Ber, the Maggid of Mezritch (d. 1772), saw a crystallization and expansion of the teachings of Chasidism. The "outreach" aspect of the Ba'al Shem Tov's teachings was never neglected by the Maggid and was, in fact, even expanded through the network of close disciples whom he sent out as emissaries to all areas of Eastern Europe. Nevertheless, chasidic teachings *per se* became developed and amplified in the teachings of the Maggid. It is beyond the scope of this work to analyze the differences between the Ba'al Shem Tov's style of delivery and the Maggid's, but even a cursory study of their respective works[1] indicates clearly that this is the case.

It was specifically in the third generation of Chasidism, however, that chasidic teachings began to be disseminated as a comprehensive system of thought. We mentioned above the story of Rabbi Shneur Zalman's imprisonment and the visit of the Ba'al Shem Tov and the Maggid of Mezritch to his prison cell. In answer to Rabbi Shneur Zalman's question as to whether he should stop revealing the esoteric teachings of Chasidism to the extent that he had been doing, when he would be released, they replied that he should not stop. On the contrary, after his release he should continue in even greater measure. There is a marked difference between the style of discourse delivered by Rabbi Shneur Zalman

---

1. Note that the Ba'al Shem Tov did not write *Keter Shem Tov* and *Tzva'at HaRibash* himself. These collections of his teachings were recorded by his disciples.

prior to his imprisonment, and subsequent to it (1799). Prior to his imprisonment, his teachings have the characteristic brevity and pithiness of the Maggid's teachings. After his imprisonment, his teachings show a marked intensification of theme and expansion of style. Many of the discourses from the latter period are accompanied by complex and highly detailed explanations drawn from kabbalistic sources. The distinction between these two periods was so clearly marked that the fifth Lubavitcher Rebbe, Rabbi Shalom Dov Ber of Lubavitch (1860–1920), referred to them as the eras "before Petersburg" and "after Petersburg."[2]

The Lubavitcher Rebbe, Rabbi M. M. Schneerson, has given a remarkable analysis of the story of Rabbi Shneur Zalman's imprisonment, which will serve to illuminate some vital points regarding the advent and rise of the *Chabad* school.[3]

The Rebbe points out that the Ba'al Shem Tov and the Maggid told Rabbi Shneur Zalman that his imprisonment was the result of a heavenly accusation, due to the extent and scope of his revelation of the esoteric wisdom. Accordingly, Rabbi Shneur Zalman himself was unsure whether he had done the right thing and whether perhaps he should cease revealing esoteric chasidic teachings if released. To this, his masters replied that he should continue in even greater measure.

This requires explanation: A heavenly accusation of the same sort had already taken place during the Maggid's reign. Chasidic tradition relates[4] that once a piece of paper on which was written some of the esoteric secrets somehow found its way to an unholy or unclean place, where it should not have been. As a result, a

---

2. *Torat Shalom* (Kehot, 1983), p. 112ff.

3. *Likkutei Sichot*, vol. 30, p. 170–175. The gist of the discourse follows.

4. *Hatamim*, vol. 2, p. 49; *Igrot Kodesh* (letters) of Rabbi J. I. Schneerson, vol. 3, p. 326 ff.

heavenly charge was brought against the Maggid for publicizing the deepest secrets of the Torah so that "the holy stones are spilled out in the public thoroughfares" (Lamentations 4:1). However, Rabbi Shneur Zalman managed to annul the accusation by means of a parable regarding a king's son who fell dangerously ill. No remedy could be found to cure the prince other than a medication made from a very rare precious stone, the only sample of which was the chief jewel in the king's crown. The stone had to be ground to a powder, mixed with water, and poured between the lips of the deathly ill prince, in the hope that the few drops he might manage to swallow would be sufficient to save his life. And so it was . . . This, too, argued Rabbi Shneur Zalman, is our case. Revealing the secrets of the Torah (the most precious jewel in the King's crown) is the only way in which the life of the prince (the Jewish people) can be saved, even if much of the remedy goes to waste.

If Rabbi Shneur Zalman was able to annul the heavenly accusation against revealing the secret teachings in the time of the Maggid, by means of the above parable, why didn't he use the same parable to nullify the accusation against himself a generation later? asks the Rebbe. Moreover, Rabbi Shneur Zalman was so plagued by doubts that he had perhaps acted incorrectly by revealing too much of the secret teachings that he had to wait for the approval of the Ba'al Shem Tov and the Maggid to continue doing so.

This can be understood, explains the Rebbe, on the basis of a comment made by R. Yitzchak Luria, the *Arizal*. He declared that "in these latter generations it is permitted and is also a *mitzvah* [in the sense of being a positive act, or perhaps even an obligation] to reveal this wisdom [the esoteric teachings of *Kabbalah*]."[5] This is despite the fact that in former generations it was concealed even

---

5. See R. Chaim Vital's introduction to *Eitz Chaim; Tanya Kuntreis Acharon*, p. 156b.

from learned Torah scholars, other than a select few possessing special abilities,[6] as will be explained at length later (chapter 3). How, then, was it permitted to reveal this wisdom in later generations, particularly in view of the principle that as the generations continue, they become less worthy, less knowledgeable, and less capable?[7]

. The Rebbe explains that it is self-understood that the preconditions and limitations on learning the esoteric aspects of the Torah are not because of any flaw in the Torah itself, but only because of the inability of those learning these subjects to fully comprehend them, to the extent that their study might cause more harm than good.[8] However, as regards the Torah itself, this esoteric wisdom is just as much a part of Torah as any other, and is in itself relevant to every Jew—for each and every Jew was granted the Torah as an inheritance.[9] Moreover, every Jew is obligated to learn these aspects of the Torah, just as he is required to learn other aspects of the Torah.[10] Furthermore, in the messianic era, the study of the esoteric aspects of the Torah ("the knowledge of God") will be the primary focus of Torah study, as Maimonides himself points out.[11]

Nevertheless, it is specifically in the latter generations that "it is permitted and a *mitzvah* to reveal this wisdom!" The Rebbe offers two explanations for this:

---

6. See Maimonides, *Code, Yesodei HaTorah*, end chap. 2; ibid. 4:11ff. This is also the authoritative decision of *Shulchan Aruch Orach Chaim*, 240. However, see *Shulchan Aruch HaRav, Hilchot Talmud Torah*, chap. 4.

7. See *Shabbat* 112b.

8. See *Yoma* 72b.

9. *De Tzva'at HaRivash*, p. 3–4 Deuteronomy 33:4. See Maimonides, *Code, Talmud Torah*, beg. chap. 3.

10. See *Shulchan Aruch HaRav, Talmud Torah*, 1:4; 2:10.

11. *Code, Melachim*, end chap. 12; *Tanya, Iggeret HaKodesh*, end chap. 26.

1. In his introduction to the *Guide for the Perplexed*, Maimonides writes that he has taken the liberty of revealing some esoteric matters on the basis of the talmudic ruling[12] that in order to act for the sake of God, it may sometimes be necessary "to 'infringe' [one of the laws] of the Torah"[13]—in this case, the prohibition against revealing the esoteric wisdom. In reality, of course, this does not constitute an infringement per se of the laws of the Torah. On the contrary, it is precisely for the sake of bolstering the Torah's authority (when this was deemed necessary by the Sages of the generation) that this was done.[14] Since Maimonides realized that many members of his generation were in a state of confusion and were being led seriously astray, he was forced to reveal certain esoteric matters in order to restore their faith. So, too, regarding the revelation of the secrets of the Torah in the latter generations—this is in the category of "infringing" one of the laws of the Torah (by revealing esoteric teachings) for the sake of arousing and strengthening the faith and practice of the Jewish people in an era of spiritual darkness and alienation.

2. There are a number of matters that serve as a preparation for the messianic era—in the words of Maimonides, "to set the Jews straight and prepare their hearts"[15] for the advent of the Messiah. Moreover, this can only be done by revealing the esoteric wisdom of the Torah, for reasons that were explained in the preceding chapter.

---

12. *Gittin* 60a.

13. Psalms 119:126.

14. This must be contrasted with the idea of making compromises in the law—an idea that is totally anathema to Orthodox Judaism.

15. *Code, Melachim* 12:2.

The Rebbe then goes on to explain that paralleling the two reasons for revealing the secrets of the Torah are two ways in which these secrets are revealed:[16]

1. Where the emphasis is on knowing the main point of the idea that is expressed in the most concise possible way, similar to the format of the *Mishnah*. Here the essential idea is expressed as an almost dimensionless point that can be understood only by the soul, but not by the intellect.
2. Where the matter is discussed and explained at length, similar to the style of talmudic dialectic. This the *Zohar*[17] refers to as "being nourished" by the secrets of Torah. That is, divine concepts are explained in a manner that can be understood intellectually, so that they become "food for the soul."[18]

Furthermore, the Rebbe argues, the way in which the secrets of Torah are revealed (either in concise form like the *Mishnah*, or at length, as in the Talmud) is a result of the reason for its revelation in the latter generations:

When the revelation of the secrets of the Torah is in the category of "infringing the general prohibition against revealing the secrets of the Torah"—for the sake of arousing and strengthening the faith and practice of the Jewish people in an era of spiritual darkness and alienation—then it is sufficient to reveal those secrets in point form, in the most concise way possible. Since this in itself is sufficient to restore the soul, no more than this may be revealed.

However, when the revelation of the secrets of the Torah is in the category of "preparing for the messianic era," at which time the

---

16. See also *Likkutei Sichot*, vol. 4, p. 1138, n. 22.
17. *Tikkunei Zohar*, end *tikkun* 6.
18. *Tanya*, chap. 5.

study of the esoteric aspects of the Torah ("the knowledge of God") will be the primary focus of Torah study, it is obvious that the preparation for that era must also be in the same manner.

On this basis, the Rebbe explains the nature of the heavenly accusation against Rabbi Shneur Zalman for revealing too much of the esoteric teachings: Whereas the Ba'al Shem Tov and the Maggid had revealed the esoteric teachings in the most concise possible manner, as almost dimensionless points, in order to save the spiritual life of the Jewish people, Rabbi Shneur Zalman revealed the esoteric teachings extensively, accompanied by detailed explanations so that they could even be understood intellectually, in order to prepare the way for the Messiah. It was precisely this difference between the teachings of his predecessors and his own teachings that galvanized a new accusation against Rabbi Shneur Zalman, and it was for this reason, too, that he was unable to nullify the accusation against himself by using the parable of the king's gravely ill son. As medication for the restoration of the soul, only a drop or two of the precious remedy—the revelation of the esoteric teachings as dimensionless points—was necessary. However, when Rabbi Shneur Zalman began to teach the innermost secrets of the Torah extensively, a new heavenly accusation was raised. The life of the prince was no longer in danger, for the teachings of the Ba'al Shem Tov and the Maggid had achieved their aim, to revive the prince and restore him to health—and, accordingly, it was forbidden to reveal the teachings to any greater extent.

When Rabbi Shneur Zalman expressed his doubts as to whether he should continue to reveal the esoteric teachings in this manner, the Ba'al Shem Tov and the Maggid replied that his self-sacrifice (*mesirut nefesh*) for the sake of setting the Jews straight and preparing their hearts for the advent of the Messiah had caused the accusation above to be annulled. Thus, the path of Rabbi Shneur Zalman was vindicated, and he was given permission to continue in even greater measure than before. It should be pointed out that this does not mean that Rabbi Shneur Zalman was simply rewarded for his *mesirut nefesh*. Rather, as a direct result of his *mesirut nefesh*, he attained the ability to reveal the secrets of the Torah, for the essence of the soul, which is bared precisely through *mesirut nefesh*,[19] is bound up with the innermost dimension of the Torah.[20]

The *Chabad* style of Chasidism was thus born. It gave those who were knowledgeable in Torah, but had not had a chasidic education, the opportunity to absorb the teachings of Chasidism without that which the opponents of Chasidism saw as the emotional excesses of a chasidic manner of worship.

From the following account of Rabbi Shneur Zalman's first encounter with the Maggid and his disciples (as recorded by the previous Lubavitcher Rebbe, Rabbi J. I. Schneersohn), it is clear that Rabbi Shneur Zalman saw his approach as the proper fulfillment of the Maggid's intention:[21]

> The Maggid's disciples[22] were discussing the various categories of angels of the Divine Chariot and their counterparts in every world. One of the disciples spoke of the angels as Abstract Intellects whose very life is the Word of God.[23] Another spoke of the celestial beings that are continually in alternating states of love and awe, of "advance and retreat."[24] Another [spoke of] even loftier beings. Several disciples discussed the *sefirot*[25] of the world of *Atzilut* . . .

---

19. See *Kuntreis Ha'avodah*, R. Shalom Dovber Schneersohn, chap. 5.

20. See *Sha'arei Orah*, R. Dovber Schneersohn, Intro.

21. *Torat HaChasidut*, Rabbi J. I. Schneersohn, chap. 8 (translated by R. Z. Posner as *On the Teachings of Chassidus* 1959).

22. In the original: The *chevraya kadisha*—(the "holy brotherhood."

23. See *Tanya, Sha'ar HaYichud v'ha'Emunah*, chap. 1.

24. *Ratzoh v'Shov*, in the original. See *Ezekiel* 1:4, Rashi.

25. *Sefirot* (Divine emanations; *Atzilut*—(the highest of the four planes of immanent reality discussed in *Kabbalah*.

The impassioned words kindled a fire of longing for God in the hearts of all the disciples. They were overwhelmed by a state of ecstasy. They moved their lips silently, trembling and weeping. Some faces were inflamed, eyes shining, hands outstretched, as though thunder-struck. Others among them were chanting inaudibly, their hearts bursting, and their souls about to expire in cleaving to their Maker. . . .

No doubt, had the Maggid not entered the hall at that moment some of the men would have simply expired as a result of their tremendous longing and desire to unite with the Almighty. But as soon as the Maggid's footsteps were heard, instantly the entire group came out of their reverie and stood, prepared to receive their master.

The Maggid took his accustomed seat at the head of the table and began: "[It is written] 'I made the earth and I created man upon it' (Isaiah 45:12). He who is the true 'I,' unknown to and concealed from the loftiest emanations, clothed His Essence within numerous condensations to give rise to emanations and creatures, the various categories of angels, and worlds without number. Through countless condensations, 'I made the earth and I created man upon it.' Man is the purpose of creation, and *barati* [the Hebrew for 'I created'], having the numerical equivalent[26] of 613 [the number of biblical commandments], is the purpose of man. The *Pardes*,[27] quoting *Sefer HaBahir*,[28] states that the attribute of kindness[29] said before the Holy One, 'Master of the Universe! Since the days of Abraham, I have no function to perform, because Abraham serves in my stead.' For Abraham, a

---

26. Each letter of the Hebrew alphabet has a numerical equivalent, called *gematria*. Computation of *gematrias* is a well-known kabbalistic device for revealing mystical allusions of words and their connection to other words or events.

27. By R. Moshe Cordovero (circa 1522–1570). This is a classic kabbalistic work systematizing the teachings of the *Kabbalah* in the tradition of the *Zohar*.

28. Attributed to one of the Sages of the mishnaic period.

29. *Chesed*, in Hebrew.

soul clothed in a body, occupied himself with hospitality to strangers as a means of disseminating the idea of God. This is higher than the attribute of kindness itself in its highest plane. The 'complaint' of the attribute of kindness was the expression of that attribute's envy of the Patriarch."

Concluding his words, the Maggid retired to his quarters. His brief discourse had a calming, quieting effect on his disciples.

Rabbi J. I. Schneersohn then explained that Rabbi Shneur Zalman became a chasid not because of the ecstasy of the angels, but because of the intellectual composure of the Maggid of Mezritch.

"He absorbed the profound concept that the highest attribute of kindness envies a man hospitable for God's sake. The Maggid's lesson teaches us the wondrous heights of man and his intellectual and moral powers. It is through the subjugation of his intellectual powers to the service of God that man becomes more exalted than the most elevated level. . . ."[30]

Moreover, the disciples were given to understand that the purpose of man is to fulfill the 613 commandments in this world, rather than attain a state of ecstasy that removes him from this world. To attain the very highest level of love of God, "the attribute of kindness in its highest plane" cannot compare to the fulfillment of the commandments on the physical plane, for within the latter, "He who is the true 'I,' unknown to and concealed from the loftiest emanations," can be grasped. (Why this is so will be explained later in this book).

---

30. *Torat HaChassidut,* ad loc., chap. 10.

3

THE ESSENCE OF CHASIDISM AND ITS CREATIVE CONTRIBUTION

Although we have discussed the advent of Chasidism and its *raison d'etre*, we must now define its purpose, and its creative contribution to Torah and Jewish life, as seen from its own point of view. Several explanations have been given:[1]

1. In the era of the Ba'al Shem Tov, the world was in a state of spiritual "unconsciousness," and through the revelations of

---

1. See *On the Essence of Chassidus*, based on a discourse delivered by the Lubavitcher Rebbe, Rabbi M. M. Schneerson, on the 19th of *Kislev* 1965, p. 1ff.

the Ba'al Shem Tov and the teachings of Chasidism, the world was aroused from this condition.[2]

2. A *chasid* is one who does more than the letter of the law requires.[3]

3. The distinctive quality of Chasidism is that one's natural faculties are transformed into Godly faculties.[4] Rabbi Shneur Zalman of Liadi, author of the *Tanya*, expressed it in the following way: The entire idea of Chasidism is to transform the nature of one's character traits.[5] This means to change not only one's natural characteristics themselves, but also the very nature of one's character.[6]

4. The teachings of Chasidism create the possibility for every person, including one who does not possess a lofty soul and who has not purified himself, to be able to grasp and comprehend Godliness.[7] By explaining the ideas of the esoteric part of the Torah and making them accessible to the intellect through examples and analogies (often taken from a person's own physical and psychological workings), Chasidism enables everyone to comprehend even this part of Torah. Moreover, not only can he grasp this with the intelligence of the divine soul that resides within him, but also with the intelligence of the intellectual soul, and even with the intellect of the animal soul.[8]

---

2. From an old Chasidic manuscript whose author is anonymous. See *Kovetz Yud Shevat*, pp. 65ff.

3. *Sefer HaMa'amarim* 5672, by R. Shalom Dovber of Lubavitch, vol. 2, pp. 772ff.

4. Ibid.

5. Recorded in *Likkutei Dibburim*, vol. 1, p. 56a.

6. Ibid., p. 56b.

7. *Torat Shalom*, p. 113.

8. The nature of each of these three souls will be explained later in the book.

5. The quintessential point of Chasidism is the effusion of a new level of light[9] from the innermost level of *keter*,[10] and from even higher—it is an effusion from the innermost level of *atik* itself,[11] which is the level of the *Ein Sof* that is found in *radla*. (These technical kabbalistic terms will be explained later. Suffice it to say that the level spoken about here is so sublime that it is entirely unknowable, not only because of its profundity, but because it is completely beyond the realm of knowledge).

Each of these explanations will now be examined briefly, shedding light on the nature of Chasidism, in general, and on the intellectual *Chabad* school of Chasidism, in particular.[12]

UNCONSCIOUSNESS

One answer to the question regarding the nature of Chasidism, in general, and its creative contribution to Torah and Jewish life, focuses on the socio-historical era of the Ba'al Shem Tov. This era is described as having been in a state of "spiritual unconsciousness." Through the revelation of the Ba'al Shem Tov and the teachings of Chasidism, the Jewish world was aroused from this condition.

When the Ba'al Shem Tov appeared on the scene, in approximately 1734, Judaism and Jewry in Eastern Europe were indeed in a desperate state. Religious, social, and economic discrimina-

---

9. *Or Hadash*, in the original.

10. *Sefer HaMa'amarim* 5672, chap. 373.

11. Ibid., chaps. 374, 376; *On the Essence of Chassidus*, p. 8ff.

12. Much of the following condensed socio-historical overview of the period is based on *Rabbi Shneur Zalman*, vol. 1, Nissan Mindel, Chabad Research Center—Kehot, Brooklyn 1980, pp. 10–13.

tion against the Jews, which had been their lot for generations, had turned into outright religious, social, and economic persecution. The average Jew was downtrodden, wretchedly poor, and in constant fear for his life. The whims and passions of tyrannical fiefs had to be paid for by the Jew. To make matters worse, since the lot of the average non-Jewish peasant also left much to be desired, a scapegoat for the world's evils had to be found.[13] Who better than the defenseless Jew? The Church, for its own reasons, turned a blind eye to the persecution, giving tacit approval to anti-Semitic outbursts. Moreover, in an untold number of cases, it was the Christian prelate who instigated anti-Jewish activities, which often culminated in vicious pogroms against the unfortunate Jews.

In the year 1648, fifty years before the birth of the Ba'al Shem Tov, the Cossack insurrection under Hetman Bogdan Chemelnicki began. The Jews were one of the prime targets of the bloodthirsty Cossacks. From the Ukraine, Cossack and Tartar hordes swept through Poland, sowing death and destruction in their path. Thousands of Jews were butchered mercilessly, and their homes and livelihoods were destroyed by the barbaric hordes.[14] For two agonizing years these atrocities—known as the *gezeirot* of *tach v'tat*[15]—went almost unchecked, until the Cossacks were finally driven back to the steppes from which they had come. The surviving Jewish communities were given no respite, however. They soon found themselves in midst of war, as the Russians and the Swedes invaded Poland. The Jews were viewed as traitors and enemies by both sides and, of course, looting and pillaging, often

---

13. See, for example, the anti-Semitic diatribes of the French philosopher, Voltaire, who never missed an opportunity to voice his invective against the Jews.

14. The eyewitness accounts of the events that took place are truly horrifying. See *HaHasidism*, Y. Alfassi, (Ma'ariv, 1977) pp. 8–9.

15. I.e., the decrees of 5408 (1648) and 5409 (1649).

ending in pogroms, was rife. Blood libels also became a common-place event.[16]

Poland was not the only country in which Jews suffered terri-bly. The Thirty Years' War (1618–48) in Central Europe devastated many communities in and around Germany, bringing economic and social ruin upon the Jews. Religious persecution in Austria was rife, and official anti-Semitism made the position of Jews in many countries extremely precarious.

Many Jews saw these events as the final cataclysm preceding the messianic era that the Prophets had foreseen and written about.

Indeed, in this fertile climate, a self-proclaimed messianic figure, Shabbetai Zevi (1626–1676), soon appeared on the scene. He declared the Chemelnicki pogroms as the "birth-pangs of the Messiah," and himself as the long-awaited redeemer. He soon gained many adherents, including some prominent rabbis, who initially supported his messianic claims. The messianic dream, however, was soon shattered by Shabbetai Zevi's antinomian behavior, which led to his eventual apostasy and conversion to Islam,[17] along with a number of his followers.

Some fifty years later, another pseudo-messianic figure emerged, in the person of Jacob Frank, a contemporary of the Ba'al Shem Tov and also a native of Podolia. Frank had become attracted to Shabbateanism in Salonika, and in 1755 he returned to his native province, where he rallied a number of the faithful around him. The debauched festivities of the sect soon came to the attention of the rabbis, who published an edict of excommunication against him. The Bishop of Kamenitz, seeing this as an opportunity to

---

16. Christian sources mention more than twenty blood libels in Poland between the years 1700–1760. *Concerning the Polish Jewish Question*, L. Smolenski, p. 29, cited in *HaHasidism*, p. 10.

17. Podolia, during the years 1672–1699, was annexed to Islamic Turkey.

attack the Jews, demanded a religious disputation between the Jews and the Frankists. The disputation was held in June 1757, and the Frankists, who had been touted as "Jews opposed to the Talmud" and as believers in the trinity and other basic Christian doctrines, were naturally declared the winners of the debate. As a result, copies of the Talmud were burned publicly. The sudden death of the bishop gave the Jews an opportunity to try and suppress the sect. However, Frank and his supporters approached the Archbishop of Lvov (Lwow) and requested a new disputation with the "talmudic" Jews. This debate was held in 1759. This time the Frankists claimed that the Jews used Christian blood for ritual purposes.[18] Of course, pogroms soon followed. Eventually, Frank and most of his sect converted to Christianity.

The aftermath of these extremely traumatic experiences was devastating. Abject poverty, fear of the hostile gentile population, and feelings of despair and abandonment flooded the people.[19]

In addition, the impoverished state of the general Jewish populace was such that free education generally could not be provided for the masses. The larger communities maintained talmudic academies (*yeshivot*), but only the select few were able to study there. The Jewish ideal of scholarship and learning thus became the domain of a select few. As material conditions grew worse, the gulf between the learned elite and the vast majority of unlearned Jews grew wider, until there was almost no common ground between them. Some of the early chasidic writers describe the ivory-tower attitude of the intellectual elite who, "instead of instructing the people as to what they should do [in terms of the

---

18. *Toldot HaTenuah HaFrankistit*, M. Balavan, vol. 1, p. 209–210, cited in *HaHasidism*, p. 10.

19. See *Sefer HaD'maot* (The Book of Tears), by R. Yom-Tov Lipman Heller, author of *Tosafot Yom-Tov*, a famous commentary on the *Mishnah*, vol. 3, p. 173. Cited in *HaHasidut*, p. 9.

practical *mitzvot*], they demonstrate the sharpness of their intellect and the breadth of their scholarship."[20]

The spiritual state of the Jews who lived in villages and small towns scattered throughout the Ukraine, Volhyn, and Podolia reached catastrophic proportions. Superstitions, amulets, astrology, and the like were rife among the unlearned Jews.[21]

Moreover, the abortive pseudo-messianic movements, particularly after the apostasy of their leaders,[22] had aroused unquenchable suspicion and mistrust within the ranks of the rabbinate towards the *Kabbalah* (the esoteric teachings of the Torah), as well as towards popular charismatic leaders. The *Kabbalah* was directly blamed for the antinomain behavior of the Shabbatean and Frankist sects. Needless to say, the study of *Kabbalah*, which had been quite popular among many rabbis and in leading talmudic academies in Poland and elsewhere,[23] fell into disrepute and became well-nigh forbidden.[24]

This grim situation can therefore be described as "unconsciousness," for the "body" of the Jewish people—that is, the ignorant masses—were almost totally unaware that they possessed a Jewish soul, while the "head" of the Jewish people—the scholarly elite—were almost totally unaware of the fact that they had a body that needed spiritual nurture and sustenance.

It was at this point that the Ba'al Shem Tov and the group of *nistarim* (itinerant mystics who kept their identities secret), of

---

20. *Toldot Ya'akov Yosef, Vayechi; Nasso.*

21. *Ma'aseh Tuviah*, by R. Tuviah HaCohen, (Yesnitz, 1721), p. 86, cited in *HaHasidism*, p. 10, n. 20.

22. Regarding their apostasy, see *Shabbatai Zevi*, by Gershom Scholem, (Princeton University Press, 1973), sect. 7; *A History of the Jewish People*, p. 768.

23. Cf., S. A Horodetzky, *Shelosh Me'ot Shanah shel Yahadut Polin* (Tel Aviv, 1946), pp. 97ff. Cited in *Rabbi Shneur Zalman*, vol. 1, p. 12.

24. See *HaHasidism*, by Aaron Marcus (Tel Aviv, 1953), p. 36, cited in *Rabbi Shneur Zalman*, vol. 1, p. 12.

which he had been appointed leader, appeared on the scene. Being acutely aware of the sorry spiritual situation of his brethren, the Ba'al Shem Tov and his colleagues traveled throughout the villages and towns of the region educating, uplifting, and revitalizing the people.[25] At the same time, a highly educated and intensely motivated underground network of *nistarim* was set up. They were to become the nuclei of the chasidic movement.

Although the Ba'al Shem Tov himself was an outstanding scholar, as were a large number of his followers, he nevertheless remained a popular teacher, never losing contact with the masses. He taught that it was the duty and privilege of every Jew to serve the Creator and that this duty embraced every aspect of daily life and was not confined to the study of Talmud exclusively, as the prevailing conception would have it. "Contemplate on the fact that everything in the world, absolutely everything, is filled with the Creator."[26] Accordingly, "Every person must serve God with all his might, for everything is for the sake of His service, and He wants to be served in all types of ways . . . [Even when] a person travels, or talks with others and is unable to learn Torah, he must cleave to the Creator in thought. . . ."[27]

He emphasized the importance of sincere and intense prayer, through which one can reach the highest levels.[28]

Absolute obedience to the Torah is of paramount importance,[29] and the study of Torah must be with the intention of cleaving to God and not simply a matter of intellectual gymnastics.[30] Ultimately, God cannot be comprehended rationally, and it is by means of emotional commitment and obedience to the Divine Will that the

---

25. See *Rabbi Shneur Zalman*, vol. 1, pp. 14–17.
26. *Tzva'at HaRivash* (Kehot), p. 26.
27. *Tzva'at HaRivash*, p. 1.
28. *Keter Shem Tov* (Kehot, 1981), p. 50.
29. *Tzva'at HaRivash*, p. 5–6; Keter Shem Tov, p. 63–64.
30. *Keter Shem Tov*, p. 13.

human being can come close to his Creator. "God desires the heart" in the performance of the _mitzvot_. Devoutness and self-surrender to God, sincere recitation of the holy words and the performance of the _mitzvot_ with the intention of cleaving to Him were enough to establish close contact with Him.[31]

No one was excluded from Divine service, despite his lack of knowledge. Moreover, the unlearned worshiper might even have an advantage over the scholar—whereas the scholar finds an outlet for his religious feelings through his prayers and the study of the Torah, which he is able to understand, the non scholar is consumed by the fire of his passionate yearning to cleave to God.[32]

The Ba'al Shem Tov also taught that Divine Providence (_hashgacha pratit_) extends not only to every human being, but also to the animal, plant, and even to the inanimate world. Not only does God oversee all of creation, every individual detail of creation is of utmost importance. How much more so is every individual Jew, who is part of His chosen people. (This will be discussed at length later).

The simple virtues that the Ba'al Shem Tov witnessed among the common folk—faith, sincerity, humility, love of one's fellow, and benevolence—were valued as real spiritual treasures. He encouraged the cultivation of these traits in word and deed. He taught that a whole life's mission might be for the sake of a single act of kindness.[33]

Above all, the Ba'al Shem Tov endeavored to instill the quality of joy in Divine service.[34] Awareness of the proximity of God at all times and in every place, knowing that God is the essence of

---

31. _Tzva'at HaRivash_, p. 4.

32. _Keter Shem Tov addenda_, p. 14–15.

33. _Likkutei Dibburim_, Rabbi J. I. Schneerson (Kehot: Brooklyn, 1957), vol. 1, p. 164; vol. 2, pp. 572, 618.

34. _Tzva'at HaRivash_, p. 8.

goodness whose benevolent providence extends to every individual and every detail of creation, and having the opportunity to serve the Creator in so many ways in daily life must give rise to a feeling of great joy in being alive and being a Jew. (Many of these concepts will be discussed in detail further on.)

The Ba'al Shem Tov's approach can be illustrated clearly by recounting some details of the *vikuach* ("debate") between Rabbi Shneur Zalman of Liadi and the leaders of the opposition camp (the *mitnagdim*), which took place in Minsk in the year 1783.[35]

The *mitnagdim* singled out two major areas in which they disagreed with the philosophy of the Ba'al Shem Tov:

1. According to the Ba'al Shem Tov, the prayers and devotions of that category of unlearned folk known as *amei ha'aretz* was also to be highly valued, even though they did not know the meaning of the words they uttered. The *mitnagdim* argued that this encouraging attitude towards the *amei ha'aretz* would make them arrogant and would seriously damage the dignity and status of the learned elite—the *Talmidei Chachamim*. Furthermore, talmudic sources[36] clearly indicate (they argued) that all calamities that beset the world are because of the *amei ha'aretz*.

2. The Ba'al Shem Tov maintained that even a master of the Talmud and a saintly *tzaddik* are required to do *teshuvah* ("repent"). This view, the *mitnagdim* argued, maligns the honor of the Torah and of Torah scholars, since repentance is appropriate only for one who has sinned.

Rabbi Shneur Zalman replied that the philosophy of the Ba'al Shem Tov is based on the biblical account of the "burning bush

---

35. See Rabbi J. I. Schneersohn, *Sefer HaSichot* 5702, p. 45ff; *Sefer HaChassidut*, vol. 2, p. 649ff.

36. See *Bava Batra*, p. 8a.

which was not consumed"—the first prophetic revelation experienced by Moses. It must be noted that this incident took place when Moses was first chosen as the leader of the Jewish people, and God's emissary, who was given the mission of taking God's chosen people out of exile. Thus, it contains a teaching for all leaders of the Jewish people:

On the verse, "An angel of God appeared [*vayera*] to him in a blaze of fire from amid the bush" (Exodus 3:2). The *Targum Onkelos* (the Aramaic translation of the Bible, which is regarded as an authoritative interpretation of the meaning of the text) renders the word *vayera* as *it'geli*—signifying "revelation". On the basis of other incidences of the usage of the Aramaic word *it'geli* (such as in Exodus 19:20 and Genesis 18:21), Rabbi Shneur Zalman (citing the exegesis of the Ba'al Shem Tov) showed that the word indicates a Divine revelation that can be experienced by recipients at various levels of spiritual advancement, including the very lowest levels, each according to his ability. Where did this Divine revelation take place? Within a bush! The Talmud compares Torah scholars to trees,[37] and the Torah itself to a blazing fire.[38] Rashi, the classical commentator on the Bible, points out that the Hebrew words for "a blaze of fire" (*b'labat aish*) signifies "the heart of the fire"—its core, where the heat is at its greatest intensity.

Therefore, the meaning of the revelation to Moses was that the bush that burned "and was not consumed" symbolized the unlearned folk, who are merely stunted bushes compared to the lofty and stately trees symbolizing the *Talmidei Chachamim*. Nevertheless, their simple sincerity and heartfelt prayers are the heart of the fire—a fire that is not consumed.

Moses' immediate response to his vision is, "I will turn aside and look at this great sight . . ." Rashi comments, "I will turn aside from here, and go over there."

---

37. See *Ta'anit* 7a.
38. See *Pesikta Zutrata, Yitro* 20:2.

The moral of the story, explained the Ba'al Shem Tov, is that the heart of the fire is to be found among the simple, unlearned, but sincere folk. The mission of the leader of the Jewish people is to find the "heart of fire" in the bush—in these folk. This is done by "turning aside from here, and going over there"—reaching out to the people. Moreover, it is the duty of even the greatest scholar and saint to stoke his own flames into a passion and an intense longing to unite with the Holy One.

This is the first explanation that Chasidism gives of its purpose and its creative contribution to Torah and Jewish life. Let us go on to the second explanation.

MORE THAN THE LETTER OF THE LAW

"A *chasid* is one who does more than the letter of the law requires." Generally, the requirements of the law are regarded as duties that are incumbent upon the Jew, whether he likes it or not. A *chasid* (in the classical sense—"a pious individual") does not regard the commandments as a yoke, but as an expression of God's love for him. He therefore wishes to respond in kind, by fulfilling the commandments with love.

The fifth Rebbe of *Chabad*-Lubavitch, Rabbi Shalom Dovber Schneersohn, explains[39] that this indicates that the person has no intentions of gaining any benefit for himself. His fulfillment of the Law, his Torah-study, and his relationships with his fellows are guided by completely altruistic intentions. Although it is perfectly permissible to pursue one's own spiritual enlightenment and strive for one's own spiritual benefits, such as entry into *Gan Eden* (Paradise) or the World to Come—moreover, this is even highly commendable—nevertheless, a *chasid* is one who reaches beyond that level and has no self-interest at all. This means that he is

---

39. *Sefer HaMa'amarim 5672*, p. 723.

willing to forfeit not only his own material gain for the sake of God, the Torah, and his fellow Jew, he is even willing to forfeit his own spiritual benefits for their sake. R. Dovber cites the example of Moses, who uttered 515 prayers[40] that he be allowed to enter the Land of Israel—not for his own sake (attaining a higher spiritual level)—but so that the Jewish people would have the ability to reveal a higher level of Godliness in the world.

In the same vein, when God threatened to obliterate the entire people for making and worshiping the golden calf, leaving only Moses from whom He promised to rebuild the Jewish people from scratch, Moses argued, "The people have committed a terrible sin by making themselves a deity of gold. Now, if You would, please forgive their sin! But if not, erase me from this book [the Torah] that You have written" (Exodus 32:31–32). The classical commentator, Rashi, explains that Moses requested that his name be removed from the entire Bible, and that he would die, so that no one could accuse him of failing to gain mercy for his people. A chasidic commentary[41] explains that Moses' reasoning was as follows: God said that He will destroy the entire Jewish people except me, from whom He will rebuild the nation. Thus, indirectly, it is because I exist that God even considers destroying the people, for I can serve as their substitute. Accordingly, let me be erased from the Torah and cease to exist, thus leaving no alternative other than to forgive them.

A *chasid* is therefore one who not only forgoes his own benefit (material or spiritual), he does not even avoid causing himself harm—as long as there is a possibility of benefiting another Jew.[42] Thus the second explanation. Now the third:

---

40. See *Da'at Zekeinim miBa'alei HaTosafot*, Deuteronomy 3:23.

41. From Rabbi Levi Yitzchak Schneerson, the father of the present Lubavitcher Rebbe, in *Likkutei Levi Yitzchak, Ki Tissa*.

42. See *Niddah* 17a, *Tosafot* ad loc. See also *Ba'er Heitev, Orach Chaim* 260:2; *Likkutei Sichot*, vol. 10, p. 248.

CHANGING ONE'S NATURE

"The distinctive quality of Chasidism is that one's natural faculties are transformed into Godly faculties." Self-refinement in chasidic
thought means transforming not only the natural characteristics
with which a person is born, but also the very nature of his
character. Rabbi Shneur Zalman of Liadi expressed it thus:[43] "The
entire point of Chasidism is that one should transform the nature
of one's *middot*." Specifically, the word *middot* is used to signify the
emotional attributes, such as love, fear, and so forth. However, in
a general sense, it refers to any definitive or limiting characteristic.

The explanation of this is as follows:[44] Chasidic writings state
that a person possesses three souls (or types of consciousness and
sources of motivation): the Godly soul, the intellectual soul, and
the natural soul. Each of these has intellectual and emotional
qualities appropriate to its nature. The natural soul is also called
the "animal soul," for all its desires and thoughts are directed
toward materialistic and animalistic ends. It is constantly preoc-
cupied with its own benefit, using its intellectual faculties to
rationalize its desires and justify its actions. The emotional
faculties of the animal soul are referred to collectively as the *yetzer
hara* (the inclination to self-indulgence and, eventually, to evil).

Regarding the animal soul, one cannot use the terms "self-
improvement" or "self-refinement." It needs to be transformed
completely. However, since this requires specialized means that
are unavailable to the individual at this stage of his Divine service,
in the interim, the natural inclinations toward evil must simply be
broken—by forcing oneself not to say that which the animal soul
wishes to say, by blocking one's ears to that which it wishes to
hear, and closing one's eyes to that which it wishes to see.

---

43. See Rabbi J. I. Schneersohn's letter in *Hatamim*, vol. 3, p. 65ff. See
also his *Likkutei Dibburim*, chap. 3, section 5, p. 52b ff.

44. Ibid.

True Divine service, however, is not in breaking, but rather in mending and rectifying (*tikkun*). This begins with the intellectual soul. The means of self-rectification is the study of chasidic thought. One must study those ideas that one can readily grasp and internalize, as well as matters that arouse the heart.

Both the Godly soul and the intellectual soul have emotional attributes, or *middot*. The *middot* of the intellectual soul have the tendency to be drawn toward that which is below it, at best the desire for self-fulfillment and self-expression. The *middot* of the Godly soul, however, are drawn toward that which is above it. Its natural tendency is thus self-transcendence.[45]

Rabbi Shneur Zalman's remark that "the entire point of Chasidism is that one should transform the nature of one's *middot*," can now be understood. This means that according to Chasidism, one is required to change the *middot* of both of these souls. As regards the intellectual soul, this means the recognition that one must do what is good and right because this is what God commanded, not because it is rationally acceptable, or because it is "good" for oneself—that is, for reasons of self-gain. As explained above, a *chasid* serves without expectation of reward.[46] As regards the *middot* of the Godly soul, whose natural desire is to rise above this world and cleave to its source in God, Chasidism demands that a person direct his *middot* toward the service of God in the physical world—through fulfilling the commandments in practice. This is known in chasidic thought as the superiority of *shov*—living properly within the world, over *ratzoh*—transcending the world.[47]

---

45. See *Tanya*, p. 35.

46. See *Avot* 1:3.

47. This will be discussed at length later on, from several points of view. See chaps. 4, 6, 11, 17.

COMPREHENDING GODLINESS

The teachings of Chasidism create the possibility for every person, including one who does not possess a lofty soul, and who has not purified himself, to be able to grasp and comprehend Godliness. By explaining the ideas of the esoteric part of the Torah, and making them accessible to the intellect, Chasidism enables everyone to comprehend even this part of Torah. Moreover, not only can he grasp this with the intelligence of the divine soul that resides within him, but also with the intelligence of the intellectual soul, and even with the intelligence of the animal soul.

There are four dimensions or levels of meaning and interpretation in the Torah:[48] *Peshat*, the "plain meaning" of the text; *remez*, "allusion," in which a deeper meaning is hinted at but not stated explicitly; *derush*, the homiletical and ethical explanation of the Torah; and *sod*, the esoteric dimension.

It must be noted that these four dimensions or levels of meaning in the Torah are four aspects of the same Torah and are inseparable from one another. The *Zohar* refers to the esoteric teachings of the Torah as "the soul of the Torah," and its exoteric teachings as "the body of the Torah."[49] Just as the body without a soul is cold and dead, so, too, say the kabbalists, is Torah-study that is not vitalized by pondering its inner dimensions.[50] Of course, the reverse also applies—study of the esoteric aspects of the Torah without the performance of the commandments makes such study "like a soul without a body—aimlessly floating about

---

48. See *Zohar Chadash Tikkunim*, 107c; ibid., 102b; *Zohar*, vol. 1, 26b; *Zohar*, vol. 3, 110a, 202a.

49. Vol. 3, p. 152a. See also R. Moshe Cordovero, *Or Ne'erav*, pt. 1, chaps. 1–2.

50. R. Chaim Vital, introduction to *Eitz Chaim*.

in a void."[51] (The importance of the performance of the practical commandments in the chasidic world view, and the danger of antinomianism will be discussed later at length).

Nevertheless, the Talmud[52] and major codifiers, including Maimonides[53] and R. Moshe Isserles[54] (the *Ramah*), rule that there are a number of preconditions and limitations proscribing learning and teaching *Kabbalah*. One of the later authorities[55] of Jewish law cites several opinions that "one should not learn *Kabbalah* . . . until the age of forty . . . particularly since sanctity, purity, alacrity, and an untainted soul are required for this." Even those who fulfilled these conditions were taught the principles of *Kabbalah* in the most discreet way, without making the matter public.[56] Moreover, kabbalistic texts themselves endorse these restrictions, as we see from the words of the *Zohar*:[57] "One may not reveal the secrets of the Torah other than to a person who is wise and has studied Scripture and Talmud, whose studies endure, and who is God-fearing and learned in everything." R. Shimon bar Yochai, the author of the *Zohar*, confirms that he was given permission to reveal the mysteries of the Torah to his colleagues only.[58] R. Shimon and his circle of disciples, known as the *chevraya kadisha* ("the holy fellowship"), are the classic representation of those whose entire occupation is Torah study.[59]

Similarly, R. Chaim Vital, the chief disciple and codifier of the *Arizal*—R. Yitzchak Luria, the famed sixteenth-century kabbalist of Safed, Israel—writes that

---

51. Ibid.
52. *Chagiga* 11bff.; Rashi.
53. *Code, Yesodei HaTorah*, end chap. 2; ibid. 4:11ff.
54. *Shulchan Aruch, Yoreh De'ah* 246:4.
55. Shach, *Shulchan Aruch, Yoreh De'ah* 246:6.
56. See *Chagiga* 11bff.
57. *Zohar Chadash, Bereishit* 6d.
58. See *Zohar*, vol. 3, 159a.
59. See *Berachot* 16b; *Shabbat* 11a; *Zohar*, vol. 3, 238b.

Man must study the wisdom of the *Kabbalah*, but first, his body must be purified. This is brought about by fulfilling the *mitzvahs* [the commandments], which serve this purpose[60] and are essential thereto. Only after this can the soul radiate in this body like a candle within a lantern—shining and invigorating him through understanding the secrets of the Torah, and revealing its depths.[61]

Several reasons are given for these restrictions. Among them: Discussing these very subtle matters in public is disrespectful toward God, as the verse states, "It is the glory of God to conceal a thing" (Proverbs 25:2);[62] it is impossible for a created being (excluding those who have reached an elevated spiritual level) to understand these matters clearly;[63] as a result of unintentional misunderstanding, one might perceive a separation in that which is absolutely unified; and so on.

Nevertheless, R. Yitzchak Luria stated that "in these latter generations, it is permitted and is also a *mitzvah* to reveal this wisdom [the esoteric teachings of *Kabbalah*]."[64] In the words of another distinguished kabbalist:[65]

The decree against open involvement with the True Wisdom [i.e., *Kabbalah*] was for a limited period of time, namely, up until the year 1490.[66] From then onwards, the decree was annulled and it is permissible to occupy oneself with the study of the *Zohar*. Since

---

60. Cf. *Bereishit Rabbah* 44:1.

61. Introduction to *Eitz Chaim*.

62. As mentioned previously in chap. 1, in the conversation of R. Levi Yitzchak of Berditchev and Rabbi Shneur Zalman of Liadi.

63. See *Kuntreis Limud HaChassidut*, Rabbi J. I. Schneersohn (Kehot, 1978), p. 3.

64. See R. Chaim Vital's introduction to *Eitz Chaim; Tanya Kuntreis Acharon*, p. 156b.

65. R. Abraham Azulai, in his introduction to *Or HaChamah*, in the name of earlier Sages.

66. The significance of this date and the one that follows is not clear.

the year 1540, it is a most commendable precept to be occupied with this study in public, for both the great and the ordinary person. It is by virtue of this merit, and no other, that the King Messiah will come in the future. It is therefore improper to be lazy in this matter.[67]

Nevertheless, even during the time of the *Arizal*, the revelation of this knowledge was not widespread. It was only with the advent of the Ba'al Shem Tov, and through his efforts, that the extensive and all-embracing dissemination of this wisdom began. This was in accordance with the response he received from the Messiah to disseminate these teachings (as explained earlier).

However, it was especially after the revelation of the intellectual branch of Chasidism,[68] the *Chabad*-Lubavitch dynasty, that these teachings were revealed in a way that can "sustain and nourish,"[69] for then Chasidism was articulated in terms of man's intellectual understanding and in rational language, which is called "food" for the soul.[70] This was particularly so after the imprisonment and subsequent release of Rabbi Shneur Zalman—"after Petersburg," as mentioned earlier. (The reason for the revelation of the esoteric teachings and the license to study and propagate them specifically

---

67. See also the ruling given by R. Yitzchak D'l'Tash, printed at the beginning of the *Zohar; Shomer Emunim vikuach* 1:29ff.

68. From a discourse given by the Lubavitcher Rebbe on the last day of Passover, 1970. (Printed as an appendix in *On the Essence of Chassidus* p. 92–94.)

69. *Tikkunei Zohar*, end of *tikkun* 6, records that Elijah the Prophet revealed to R. Shimon bar Yochai that "many people below will be sustained and nourished from this work of yours [the *Zohar*] when it will be revealed below in the latter generations, at the end of days." On its account, the messianic redemption will come about. *Kiseh Melech* (ad loc) explains that this means that the *Zohar's* profound teachings will be clearly explained and properly understood.

70. See *Tanya*, end of chap. 5.

in the latter generations was discussed more fully in the previous
chapter).

What is the methodology of Chasidism that enables it to reveal
the ideas of the esoteric part of the Torah, "and make them
accessible to the intelligence of the intellectual soul, and even to
the intelligence of the animal soul," so that even ordinary people
who do not possess lofty souls and have not purified themselves
"will be able to make unifications and ascents of soul" just like the
greatest saints?

Rabbi Shalom Dov-Ber of Lubavitch (1860–1920), the fifth
Lubavitcher Rebbe, explains[71] that although the content and
subject matter of chasidic meditation is primarily the kabbalistic
writings of the Arizal, nevertheless, the methodology of their
study is very different from the traditional methods of speculative
Kabbalah.[72] The basis of Kabbalah is the verse in Ezekiel's vision
of the Divine Chariot—"Upon the Throne was the appearance of
the likeness of Man" (Ezekiel 1:21). In the writings of the Arizal,
Godliness has thus been "clothed" in "the likeness of man," that
is, abstract divine matters are made accessible to human understanding by depicting them in human terms and images, allowing
the mind to grasp what is essentially beyond human comprehension. The writings of the Arizal are indeed replete with anthropomorphic terminology and imagery. For example: The sefirah
("divine emanation") of chochmah ("wisdom") is referred to as
abba ("father"). The sefirah of binah is referred to as imah
("mother"). The interaction of these two sefirot is known as zivug
("coupling" or "union"). The products of this union are ben ("son",
referring to the configuration of six sefirot, from chesed to yesod)

---

71. *Torat Shalom*, p. 255ff. What follows is a paraphrase and explanation of his speech on the occasion of the 19th of Kislev 5669 (1909).

72. There are two main fields of Kabbalah—(*Kabbalah ma'asit* ("practical *Kabbalah*"), which is not in the scope of the present discussion at all;
Kabbalah iunit—"speculative Kabbalah," or kabbalistic theory.

and *bat* ("daughter", the *sefirah* of *malchut*), and so on. Of course, these terms should not be taken at face value. The intention is only to understand Godliness by way of human metaphors, as the Sages of the Talmud noted: "The Torah speaks in the language of man,"[73] in order to make abstract concepts comprehensible to the human mind. Nevertheless, divine emanations are depicted in human terms.

The methodology of Chasidism, however, is exactly the opposite. Chasidic philosophy is based on the verse, "We shall make man in Our image" (Genesis 1:26). Since man is the reflection of the divine realm, proper scrutiny of the human realm leads to understanding of the divine realm. Moreover, the human realm is easily accessible to all, and understanding of it does not require a special level of sanctity and lengthy preparations and purifications. After proper introspection, by stripping the soul's qualities of their human connotations, one may have a clear view of the divine realm. By understanding the operation of the faculties of one's own soul—such as *chochmah*, *binah*, and *da'at*—one can come to an understanding of *chochmah*, *binah*, and *da'at* above. Chasidism thus uses the method of abstraction rather than anthropomorphism. Put somewhat differently, *Kabbalah* defines (and thus delimits) Godliness, by "clothing Godliness within a human form." Chasidism, by contrast, endeavors to strip away the corporeal and human aspects of the faculties of one's soul, and in this way come to an understanding of abstract and unformed Godliness, as the verse states, "From my flesh I see God"[74] (Job 19:26). Consequently, it is possible to apprehend far loftier levels of Godliness—those levels that cannot be clothed in human terms—than can be understood through traditional *Kabbalah*. Moreover, this process of teaching oneself to see Godliness

---

73. *Berachot* 31b. See also *Mechilta* and *Tanchuma* on Exodus 15:7, 19:18.

74. See also *On the Essence of Chassidus*, p. 5.

through the soul's faculties has the effect of making these faculties themselves Godly. (Note that this recalls the previous definition of the contribution and innovation of Chasidism—that it changes the nature of one's character, making it Godly).

A NEW LEVEL OF LIGHT

Although the previous four explanations of Chasidism are all correct, the Lubavitcher Rebbe declares, nevertheless, they do not describe its quintessential point, "which is completely abstracted and removed from any specific definitions." On the contrary, he adds, "it is by virtue of this quintessential point that all the above-mentioned special qualities exist and are derived."

The fifth and final definition of the essence of Chasidism offered by the Rebbe is that Chasidism is "the effusion of a new light from the innermost level of *keter*, and from even higher—it is an effusion from the innermost level of *atik* itself, which is the level of the *Ein Sof* that is found in *radla*."

Before we explain the import of the above, we must first understand the terms used. In kabbalistic terminology, *keter* ("crown") denotes the most sublime of all of the *sefirot*, or Divine emanations through which Godliness is progressively manifested[75] and which constitute the inner structure of each of the worlds, somewhat as the bones give shape and form to the human body. The term *keter* itself denotes its significance—just as a crown is placed upon the head and encompasses it, so, too, *keter* is above all of the *sefirot* and encompasses them all. The analogy may be carried further—just as the crown is neither a part of the head nor the body but is distinct from it, so *keter* is essentially

---

75. The following is based on *Mystical Concepts in Chasidism*, Rabbi J. I. Schochet, chap. 3. para. 3.

distinct from the other *sefirot*.[76] It is the first emanation, and as such is regarded as the "lowest level," so to speak, of the Emanator.[77] It is for this reason that *keter* is referred to as *temira d'chol temirin* ("the most hidden of all"),[78] and is referred to as *ayin* ("nothingness").[79] These terms signify the total concealment of the rank of *keter*, due to its supreme sublimity.

In *keter* itself there are three levels, called: *arich anpin; atik* (or *atik yomin*); and *radla*, an acronym for *reishit d'lo ityada*—"the beginning which is unknown." The lowest level of *keter*, *arich anpin*, is the lowest level of the Infinite Light (the *Or Ein Sof*—the infinite revelation of God) and from it issue forth all the other *sefirot*. Thus, in a sense, *arich anpin* is the "intermediary" between the *Or Ein Sof* and the *sefirot*.[80] *Atik*, however, is an even higher level than this. The word itself means "separated" or "removed," for it is completely removed from the *sefirot* and creation. Whereas *arich anpin* is called *ratzon ha'elyon*—"the Supernal Will of God",[81] which is manifested in His will to create—*atik* represents the internal aspect of God's will, that which motivates His will. Both of them, however, are aspects of the *Or Ein Sof*, *arich* being the external aspect and *atik* the internal aspect. *Radla* transcends even these levels. It is the *Or Ein Sof* itself.

Accordingly, when the Rebbe declares that Chasidism is the "effusion of a new light from . . . the innermost level of *Atik* itself, which is the level of the *Ein Sof* that is found in *radla*," this means that "it is completely united with the *Or Ein Sof*, which is clothed within it in a perfect and total unity."[82] Although this is

---

76. *Eitz Chaim* 25:5, 42:1.

77. Ibid.

78. *Zohar*, vol. 1, 147a.

79. *Zohar*, vol. 3, 256b.

80. See *Tanya, Iggeret HaKodesh*, chaps. 17, 20, 29.

81. *Zohar*, vol. 3, 129a, 288b.

82. *Tanya, Kuntreis Acharon*, p. 160b; *Derech Mitzevotecha*, p. 41a–b.

true of all parts of the Torah, nevertheless, the primary expression of this point is in chasidic philosophy.[83]

The reason for this is that the *Ein Sof*, which is found in all other parts of the Torah, is clothed in a certain form, a form that defines and "expresses" the nature of that part. The form of that particular part of the Torah (*peshat, remez, derush*, and *sod*) conceals the unformed abstractness of the *Ein Sof* that is clothed therein.[84] Chasidic teachings, however, are not bounded and defined by any specific form, although they can be presented through any of these forms, and they therefore do not conceal the unformed abstractness of the *Ein Sof* within. Chasidic teachings thus constitute a direct revelation of Godliness, accessible to the human mind, even when the person studying them does not possess a lofty soul and has not reached the level of purity of the great prophets and saints of Jewish history.

According to all of the above, it is clear that chasidic teachings view their purpose and their creative contribution to Torah and Jewish life as multidimensional. Historically, they functioned, and continue to function, as an antidote to spiritual "unconsciousness." In the religious dimension, Chasidism signifies a move to greater piety—swimming against the stream of religious entropy. Due to these two factors, Chasidism has been defined by some as a revivalist movement.

From a more mystical point of view, the distinctive quality of Chasidism is that it effects a spiritual transformation in the individual—one's natural faculties are transformed into Godly faculties. Furthermore, according to chasidic teachings, this ideal is not only the fervent aspiration of a select coterie of mystical seekers; the teachings of Chasidism create the possibility for every person, including one who does not possess a lofty soul and who has not purified himself, to be able to grasp and comprehend Godliness. The

---

83. *On the Essence of Chassidus*, p. 13.
84. Ibid.

methodology used is to make the most esoteric parts of the Torah accessible to the ordinary intellect through examples and analogies, thus allowing the ordinary individual to comprehend Godliness. In addition to the spiritual consequences of this, there are also social consequences, for the scholarly elite no longer have exclusive access to Divine proximity. This, again, was one of the main gripes of the *mitnagdim* against Chasidism.

From the Divine point of view, the quintessential point of Chasidism is an effusion of a new, and extremely sublime, level of light into existence. The very fact that God not only "approved" of these revolutionary events but was actually their initiator, bestowing the revelation of this level of light on existence, gave Chasidism the sanction to take the Eastern European world, and eventually almost the entire world, by storm.

4

THE PATHS OF CHAKIRA, MUSSAR, AND CHASIDISM

We mentioned previously that Jewish mysticism teaches that the purpose of the soul's descent to earth is to reveal the inherent harmony of body and soul. It was pointed out that this is achieved by teaching the soul how to recognize the spirituality of matter, and that in every physical thing, even in the inanimate, there is a "soul," which is the creative force that has brought it into being out of absolute nothingness and that continuously keeps from reverting back to its former state of nonexistence. It is this "spark" of Godliness that is the true essence and reality of all things, and this spark is released and revealed when physical matter is used for a sublime purpose or deed in accordance with the Will of the Creator, as it is in the performance of a commandment.

Chasidic texts explain that attaining the predominance of form over matter, of soul over body, involves three stages of endeavor—the subjugation and rejection of matter; cognizance of the virtue of the spiritual and cultivating an inclination toward it; and finally, mastery of form over matter.[1]

These three types of endeavor correspond to three schools of Jewish thought, all of which lead to recognition of the Creator and serving Him through Torah study and fulfilling His commandments (the *mitzvahs*). Nevertheless, each school of thought has its own distinctive methodology:

1. One approach emphasizes the subjugation of matter and demonstrates its unworthiness;
2. A second approach accentuates the recognition of the qualities of the spiritual, with the understanding that it is the basis of all physical existence;
3. A third approach concentrates on cultivating the mastery of form over matter. This, in turn, is subdivided into two categories: (a) sublimation and purification of matter to render it compatible with form, and (b) emphasis on the quality of form as embodied in matter.[2]

Although all three types of endeavor ultimately strive for the same goal, they are nevertheless three distinct schools of thought. The first of these, the school of *Mussar* (meaning literally, "ethical rebuke"), emphasizes the subjection of the material and demonstrates its unworthy grossness, including any improper propensities one might possess, such as overindulgence in food and drink and other physical passions that man shares with animals. When a man conducts himself like an animal, he lowers himself to a level below that of animals. The latter lack reason to desire anything more than the gratification of physical needs. Man, however, is endowed with intelligence to aspire to something higher, to moral virtue and to intellectual values. When he opts

---

1. Kuntreis, *Torat HaChassidut*, chap. 11.
2. Ibid.

for physical pleasures, he shows himself to be more degenerate than the animal who naturally acts this way. The school of *Mussar* thus describes the baseness of physical passions and pleasures and depicts the dire consequences that will be the lot of those who wallow in self-indulgence and the personal and social defects that accompany it.[3]

The second school of thought, theological philosophy, or *Chakira* (meaning literally, "intellectual inquiry"), stresses the qualities of the spiritual, of morality and intellect. It teaches the means of attaining these higher goals, exalting them as the basis of perfection and the aim of creation, making this world a fitting fulfillment of God's desire for "a home in the lower worlds."[4]

The third school of thought is that of Chasidism. It expounds the inherent superiority of form over matter and emphasizes the value of purified matter (physical matter that is dedicated to a higher, spiritual purpose, thus ceasing to be "merely" physical). It also accentuates the value of form when embodied in matter, producing an inseparable and harmonious union in which physical matter is elevated by its association with the spiritual, and the spiritual is fulfilled and actualized by its association with the physical, so that it no longer remains "merely" ethereal. In this union of form and matter, there is no beginning or end, superior and inferior. Each is essential to the other, and each is implanted within the other. One God created them both for the identical purpose—to reveal Godliness within existence, which can only be achieved when they exist in perfect unity.[5]

Chasidism declares that "no place is devoid of Him,"[6] and "no thought can grasp Him."[7] *Chabad* Chasidism, for example,

---

3. Ibid., chap. 12.
4. Ibid.
5. Ibid.
6. *Tikkunei Zohar*, *tikkun* 57, p. 91b.
7. *Tikkunei Zohar*, Introduction.

explains at length, using many different analytical examples, both positive[8] and negative,[9] how "no place is devoid of Him." Even though "no thought can grasp Him," nevertheless, it is each individual's duty to ponder Divine Wisdom, and understand it and explain it to himself to the maximum extent that his intellect can attain, as the verse states, "Know this day and take it to your heart . . ." (Deuteronomy 4:39).[10]

The differences between the schools of *Mussar* and Chasidism have been examined from many different angles. Referring to the verse "Turn away from evil, and do good" (Psalms 34:15), Rabbi Menachem M. Schneerson explains[11] that these represent two types of Divine service. The school of *Mussar* is based primarily on the aspect of "Turning away from evil" by emphasizing how "bad and bitter is your abandoning of the Lord your God."[12] It stresses how evil the *yetzer hara* (the evil urge) is, and it seeks to drive it out through fasts and self-inflicted suffering.

The school of Chasidism, on the other hand, is occupied primarily with contemplating the good. It explains the bountiful goodness of God and the loftiness of the soul. When a person is aware of this and appreciates it, he naturally has less affinity to wrong and to evil. The distinct advantage of this methodology is that his contemplation of the divinity and the loftiness of his own soul illuminates his entire being and raises him to a higher spiritual level. This does not happen with the methodology of *Mussar*. On the contrary, since *Mussar* concentrates on smashing the passions of the animal soul, a person is consciously occupied primarily with the negative aspects of his being—his animal soul.

---

8. I.e., describing what it is.

9. I.e., describing what it is not.

10. Part of a letter from Rabbi J. I. Schneersohn, printed in *Hatamim*, p. 291. See also *Likkutei Dibburim*, pp. 1321–1322.

11. *Likkutei Sichot*, vol. 2, p. 473ff.

12. Jeremiah 2:19.

The difference between *Mussar* and Chasidism can be explained further by way of a parable:[13] When a thief (the evil urge) comes to burgle a house, there are two ways of chasing him away. One is by shouting and making a loud noise. This will scare him away temporarily, but he is nevertheless likely to return when things have quieted down, or when he gets used to the cry of "wolf". Alternatively, one may catch the thief and even turn him into a penitent. The former, of course, corresponds to the methodology of *Mussar*, which kicks up a tremendous hullabaloo when the *yetzer hara* so much as stirs. However, since it may become immune to such measures, the second method, that of Chasidism, is to be preferred, for if the "thief" becomes a penitent, one surely has nothing to fear from him.

Another explanation: Both *Mussar* and Chasidism maintain that the Godly life-force, which creates and animates all of creation and the soul, is primary, whereas the physical body and the material world are secondary. However, *Mussar* emphasizes the inferiority of the world and the human body, whereas Chasidism emphasizes the superiority of the soul and the Godly life-force.[14] Thus, for example, *Mussar* teaches one how not to eat, whereas Chasidism teaches one what to eat and how to eat;[15] *Mussar* works tell a person to abstain and withdraw from the commercial world, whereas Chasidism teaches that one can be involved in business, for business does not contradict Divine service, since "you shall know Him in all your ways" (Proverbs 3:6).[16]

As for the difference between *Chakira* and Chasidism, this may be explained as follows: If one makes philosophical inquiry into those matters that pertain to faith alone, one is liable to be left with unanswered questions. This can easily weaken a person's

---

13. *Likkutei Sichot*, ad loc., p. 474; vol. 20, p. 608.
14. Rabbi J. I. Schneersohn, *Igrot Kodesh*, vol. 3, pp. 547–548.
15. *Hatamim*, vol. 5, p. 584ff.
16. *Torat Shalom*, p. 7.

faith, "so that the end product of such inquiry may lead a person to remove his head covering and four-cornered fringed garment.[17] But when one learns Chasidism, in the end one winds a prayer-belt around one's waist, and dons a head covering. This is because people generally learn *Chakira* with the cold intellectualism of he who rejects the yoke of heaven, whereas people generally approach the study of Chasidism with the warmth of faith, and with the acceptance of the yoke of heaven."[18]

17. His *tallit kattan*, in the original. This is a four-cornered, fringed garment worn by men under the clothes, in fulfillment of the verse "and they shall make for themselves fringes on the corners of their garments" (Numbers 15:38).

18. Rabbi J. I. Schneersohn, *Iggrot Kodesh*, vol. 4, p. 166.

2
CHASIDIC MYSTICAL THEOLOGY

5

THE ESSENCE AND THE
OR EIN SOF

Although we have outlined some of the methodological aspects of the chasidic movement, we have not yet clarified its ontological and teleological positions. The nature of the Divine Being, the purpose of creation, and the mission of man occupy a major portion of chasidic literature.

However, before these subjects can be approached, it must be pointed out that any attempt to characterize the nature of an existence that completely transcends human experience is obviously bound to use metaphors that may have anthropomorphic connotations. It is possibly for this reason that R. Chaim Vital declared that he had no license to probe beyond the inner dimensions of the transcendental plane of reality known in *Kabbalah* as *Adam Kadmon*.[1] This level is the first plane of reality to be created after the *tzimtzum*—the act whereby God limits His revelation of His infinity, allowing the initial coming-into-being of existence,

---

1. See beginning of *Otzrot Chaim*.

which, in some sense, is a limitation of the divine revelation.[2] Although it is appropriate to speak of lower levels of creation in human terms, since they are in some way accessible to the human mind and to human experience, the inner dimension of *Adam Kadmon* is so sublime that it can never be fathomed by human thought at all. Accordingly, the human terms used in *Kabbalah* may not be applied to this level without degrading its sublimity and causing a possibly fatal error in understanding the noncorporeality of the Divine.

However, the major portion of chasidic ontology and cosmology—particularly in the literature of the *Chabad* school— examines precisely those areas that precede the *tzimtzum*. The authorization for doing so, despite the stiff opposition that this aroused among the opponents of Chasidism, and even among the ranks of the chasidim themselves,[3] was presumably the conversation that the Ba'al Shem Tov had with the Messiah, as described in the first chapter, and Rabbi Shneur Zalman of Liadi's subsequent vision of the Ba'al Shem Tov, and the Maggid of Mezritch, who endorsed his system, as discussed in chapter 2. True to their credo, the *Chabad* Rebbes make every attempt to make even these matters comprehensible to the human mind. Thus, the levels of Divinity that precede the *tzimtzum* are examined at length and are clearly delineated, often using analogies drawn from the mundane world.

Before continuing with the description of the levels that precede the *tzimtzum*, a distinction must be made between the essence of God Himself, referred to in *Chabad* literature as *Atzmut*—and His revelation of His infinity, referred to as the *Or*

---

2. The concept of *tzimtzum* and the different planes of reality resulting from it will be explained at length in chapter 6.

3. Especially R. Abraham of Kalisk, R. Baruch of Mezibuz, R. Asher of Stolin, and R. Zvi Hirsch of Zydachov. See *Beit Rebbe*, pp. 162, 164–170, 172–178, 184–187, 192; *Communicating the Infinite*, p. 35ff.

Ein Sof ("the Infinite Light").[4] The terms used to describe God's unknowable Essence[5] are of necessity recondite and elliptical and, even in *Chabad* literature, are left in more or less axiomatic form.[6]

ATZMUT

Prior to the creation, God alone existed.[7] His existence is of His Essence, and, consequently, He is the only "true" existence— in other words, the only existence that is totally independent of any other existence. Thus, His existence is called "necessary existence"—that is, His being is of His Essence and is not derived from another existence that preceded Him.[8] On the contrary, He is the pre-existent Being who has no beginning and no end, and upon whom all the rest of existence is dependent.[9] In this regard, *Chovat HaLevavot*[10] states, His existence is eternal and always was, and One who always existed has no beginning.[11]

His Being is not existence in the regular sense of the word, for

---

4. See Shochet, *Mystical Concepts in Chasidism*, chap. 2.

5. Cf., God's retort to Moses, "No man shall see Me and live . . ." (Exodus 33:20).

6. Note that some of these statements are drawn from the writings of earlier authorities, such as Maimonides, Nachmanides, and Rabbeinu Bechaye.

7. See *Pirkei d' R. Elazar* 3:8.

8. See *Pirush* to Maimonides' *Yesodei HaTorah* 1:3; *Sefer HaMa'amarim 5677*, pp. 72–73.

9. *Derech Mitzevotecha*, pp. 46b, 57a; *Sefer HaMa'amarim 5666*, p. 169; *Sefer HaMa'amarim 5677*, pp. 72–73.

10. *Sha'ar HaYichud*, chap. 10. This work was written by Rabbeinu Bechaye ibn Pakuda in the year 1161.

11. Cited in *Sefer HaMa'amarim 5668*, p. 191; *Sefer HaMa'amarim 5666*, p. 343-344. See also *Derech Mitzevotecha*, p. 57a.

His existence cannot be observed or delimited so that we can say what He is[12] and in exactly what way He is superior or transcendent.[13] Rather, His existence is only that He is whatever He truly is.[14] His existence is completely uncompounded and formless,[15] and therefore bears opposites such as oneness and multiplicity, finite and infinite,[16] without these being contradictory at all.[17]

God is everywhere as He is in Himself, and no place is devoid of Him.[18] He is neither hidden nor revealed, and accordingly, everyone is aware of the existence of God, without anyone being able to comprehend Him.[19] In the words of the *Tikkunei Zohar*, He is "exalted above all heights, and hidden beyond all levels of concealment. No thought can grasp You at all . . ."[20]

Since *Atzmut* is not in the category of revelation, no descriptive terms apply to Him at all, even such lofty terms as "without a beginning," "infinite and without end [*Ein Sof*]," "First Cause,"

---

12. See Maimonides' *Moreh Nevuchin*, pt. 1, chap. 57.

13. *Sefer HaMa'amarim 5677*, R. Shalom Dov Ber Schneersohn, p. 74.

14. *Derech Mitzevotecha*, R. Menachem Mendel of Lubavitch (the *Tzemach Tzedek*) *Shoresh Mitzvat HaTefilah*, chap. 1; *Sefer HaMa'amarim 5672*, R. Shalom Dov Ber Schneersohn, pp. 560, 1144; *Sefer HaMa'amarim 5666*, R. Shalom Dov Ber Schneersohn, pp. 167–168, 172.

15. *Pashut b'tachlit hapeshitut*, in the original. *Derech Mitzevotecha*, p. 46b.

16. *Likkutei Sichot*, vol. 12, pp. 74–75, n. 25, 30; *Sefer HaMa'amarim 5672*, p. 1191.

17. *Sefer HaMa'amarim 5672*, pp. 560, 675; *Sefer HaMa'amarim 5678*, pp. 419–420.

18. *Tikkunei Zohar, tikkun 57*, p. 91b; *Tanya*, chaps. 21, 40, 51, etc.

19. *Torah Or, Patach Eliyahu*, p. 14b; *Sefer HaMa'amarim 5672*, p. 277.

20. Introduction, p. 17a–b.

and so on.[21] On the other hand, neither can anything be negated regarding *Atzmut*, for He bears all things and yet is none of them at the same time.[22]

The question is, how do we reconcile this ineffable *Atzmut* with the finite universe, the Oneness of God and the existence of multiplicity, and so on. Jewish philosophers[23] and kabbalists[24] alike have tackled this problem. Among the solutions that they have offered are what are called "intermediate agency" and "emanationism"—in other words, that creation came into being by way of a series of intermediate steps that emanated from the Creator, which place a sufficiently great distance between Him and that which He created so that the corporeality and the multiplicity of the latter are disassociated and set apart from God Himself, "who is not physical and is not affected by physical phenomena."[25] In other words, the creation came about by way of a long chain of evolutionary processes, a chain of cause and effect, that emanated from the Creator as the First (and very distant) Cause, until eventually the corporeality of this material world came into being.

R. Moshe Cordovero[26] (better known by the acronym of his name, *Ramak*) points out that this position is necessary in order to avoid the implication of a direct continuity between the Creator and the created. Accordingly, *Ramak* argues that there are a series of intermediate steps—the ten *sefirot*, including *keter*—that are produced by the Creator and that provide a gradual descent from the transcendent infinity of *Atzmut* to the plane of immanent, finite being. *Keter* is thus not the Creator Himself, but the first

---

21. See *Mishnat Chabad—Sefer HaArachim HaKatzar, Atzmut*, para. 8ff.

22. Ibid., para. 16.

23. Cf., Maimonides' *Guide*, part 2, chaps. 4–12.

24. Cf., Moshe Cordovero's *Pardes Rimonim* 4:9.

25. The third of Maimonides' Thirteen Principles.

26. *Pardes, sha'ar* 3, chap. 1.

link in finite being. Each succeeding *sefirah* from *keter* downward represents a descending level of spirituality, a series of causes and effects in which each successive level emanates from the previous level, until the lowest of the *sefirot*, *malchut*, eventually evolves. The actual creation comes about only from the level of *malchut*. Thus, a sufficiently great distance has been placed between Him and that which He created. Corporeality and the multiplicity of creation is disassociated and set apart from God Himself.

However, chasidic texts point out that *Ramak's* solution does not solve the problem. The question as to how, and at what point, the transition from infinite to finite takes place has not been answered, for as long as there is some causal relationship between the Creator and the created, between the first link in the evolutionary chain and the last, no matter how long the chain might be, there always remains some association between one level and another, and thus between the first link and the last.[27] Accordingly, the aspect of infinity is never completely extinguished. On the contrary, each successive level of being "inherits" the infinity of its predecessor, precisely because it has emanated from or has been produced by the previous level, so that finite material being could never have been created from infinite spiritual being, no matter how many causes and effects interpose between the Creator and the created.

Rabbi Isaac Luria, the *Arizal*, therefore examined the doctrine of *tzimtzum*.[28] In the *Arizal's* view, the process of creation was neither an uninterrupted sequence of causes and effects nor a gradual descent of emanations. Rather, the primary act of creation was to establish a "gap" between the Creator and the created, a "quantum leap" (*dilug*) that breaks the gradualism and establishes

---

27. *Tanya*, chap. 48; *Tanya, Iggeret HaKodesh*, chap. 20; *Likkutei Torah, Devarim*, pp. 46c, 20d.

28. See the beginning of *Eitz Chaim, Otzrot Chaim, Mevoh Shearim*, etc.

a radical distinction between the First Cause and all subsequent effects.[29] This is called the *tzimtzum.* The doctrine of *tzimtzum* was expounded by the *Arizal* in the following way: Before the universe was created, there was only the Infinite One, whose infinity filled all of existence. Within this infinity there was no place (i.e., possibility) for finite existence. But when it arose in God's will to create finite worlds, He withdrew Himself from the place where the finite worlds would be created in order to create a void (*chalal*) wherein finite existence could exist. Finite being then came about by means of a reintroduction of finite light into the void.[30]

Although we have solved the problem of arriving at finitude, we are now faced with another problem: If God withdrew Himself from the void by way of the *tzimtzum,* the creation that exists within the void is devoid of God's essence—of *Atzmut.* Moreover, this also implies a change within God, for prior to the creation He was everywhere and after the creation there is one place where He is not—the void. This violates a basic principle of Judaism—that the creation does not bring about any change whatsoever in God: "I, God, have not changed" (Malachi 3:6).

THE *OR EIN SOF*

Chabad philosophy, amplifying on a theme implicit in the writings of the *Arizal,*[31] therefore proposes a solution to these problems: Besides the Essence of God, there is another infinite existence—

---

29. See *Torah Or, Esther* 90a, 116c; *Likkutei Torah, Shir HaShirim* 40b ff., 41d, 42b ff.

30. See the beginning of *Etz Chaim, Otzrot Chaim, Mevoh Shearim,* etc.; *Tanya,* chaps. 21, 48, 49; *Likkutei Torah Vayikra,* p. 51b ff., and, especially, 52c.

31. The *Arizal* himself does not explain the concept of the *Or Ein Sof*

the "Infinite Light," or *Or Ein Sof*, which is infinite only because it is "like the Luminary [*Ma'or*]" from which it issues forth, although it is not the *Ma'or*.[32] (In this context, although not in every context, the term *Ma'or* is a metaphor for the source of the *Or Ein Sof*, the Infinite Light, and is not synonymous with *Atzmut*).

That is to say, the *Or Ein Sof* is not infinite in and of itself, for it has a beginning[33] (not a chronological beginning, but a source from whence it issues—the *Ma'or*),[34] and anything that has a beginning also necessarily has an end. Thus, it is not *Ein Sof* in itself but because it is the will of the Creator that the *Or* is like the *Ma'or*[35]—infinite (*Ein Sof*). It is for this reason that it is referred to as the *Or Ein Sof*—"the Infinite Light."

In view of the above, the following question may be asked: Since "the light is like the Luminary," which is not in the category of revelation at all, how does the *Or Ein Sof* actually become revealed?[36] *Chabad* texts explain that in order for the *Or Ein Sof* to issue forth, a very powerful act of self-restraint,[37] referred to as *ha-akava*[38] ("withholding"), took place. This may be understood by way of the following analogy: In order for a teacher to

---

at length, although many of the conclusions drawn explicitly in *Chabad* literature are implicit in the teachings of the *Arizal*.

32. *Likkutei Torah, Pikudei*, p. 7b; *Behar*, pp. 42a, 50bff; *Sefer HaMa'amarim 5666*, p. 161ff.

33. *Torat Chaim, Shemot*, p. 77a; *Or HaTorah Bamidbar*, p. 1439; *Sefer HaMa'amarim 5666*, p. 165ff.

34. *Or HaTorah Bamidbar*, p. 1439; *Biurei HaZohar* (*Tzemach Tzedek*), pp. 611–612; *Sefer HaMa'amarim 5664*, p. 159; *Sefer HaMa'amarim 5670*, p. 184.

35. *Sefer HaMa'amarim 5666*, p. 167ff; references in previous footnote.

36. Regarding the following, see *Mishnat Chabad—Sefer HaArachim HaKatzar, Tzimtzum*, chap. 1.

37. It is referred to as "similar to the *tzimtzum*," even though it precedes the *tzimtzum* mentioned in the writings of the *Arizal*.

38. *Sefer HaMa'amarim 5678*, pp. 101ff; *Sefer HaMa'amarim, Kuntreisim*,

enlighten is student, he must first "reduce" his own comprehension of the subject to be taught so that he can produce a lower-level, less powerful revelation—in our case, the *Or Ein Sof*.

The necessity for this act of "self-restraint" is explained in several ways:

By way of the *ha-akava*, the teacher (by way of analogy) conceals his overwhelming superiority over his students so that his knowledge can have some degree of relevance to them. Furthermore, the process of self-restraint also enables him to slow down his stream of inner thought so that he can find a format for his teachings that will be understood by the students. As the stream of inner thought is deliberately slowed down, the various levels of light of the *Or Ein Sof* are produced. This may be compared to refracting a ray of light through a prism in order to produce visible colors, or making sound-waves audible to the human ear by increasing or decreasing their wavelength.

The innovation of this idea is that even the very highest level of *Or Ein Sof*, way before the level of *Or Ein Sof* affected by the *tzimtzum* mentioned in the writings of the *Arizal* (as will be explained below), is also produced by a prior cause, of which it is merely the effect. That is to say, it is not produced *ex nihilo*. In other words, the *Or Ein Sof* is not a "thing" (or "object")—it is an act that must be constantly renewed in order for it to exist. The corollary of this is that the *Or Ein Sof* therefore remains "like the Luminary," for an effect always partakes of the nature of its cause.

Since the Emanator of the *Or Ein Sof* could clearly repeal this act of self-restraint, it is clear that the *Or Ein Sof* issues forth from the *Ma'or* only by the will of God, and not involuntarily.[39]

---

vol. 1, p. 209a; *Likkutei Sichot*, vol. 7, p. 89ff. See also *Torat Shalom*, p. 147. In the writings of R. Aharon of Staroselye, this is called *beki'ah*.

39. *Likkutei Torah Shir HaShirim*, p. 1b; *Derech Mitzevotcha*, p. 135b; *Sefer HaMa'amarim 5666*, pp. 169ff. See, at length, *Sefer HaArachim*, vol. 3, p. 64ff. In this sense, the analogy of the sun and the light it emits is

Therefore, the *Or Ein Sof* is totally contingent upon the *Ma'or* and would not exist at all were it not for the will of the Creator. Moreover, even after the *Or Ein Sof* has issued forth from the *Ma'or*, it continues to exist only as long as God wills it to.[40] The *Or Ein Sof* is thus described as "cleaving to the Ma'or,"[41] and it does not exist as a separate entity at all, even after it has issued forth from the *Ma'or*.[42] Thus, its existence is entirely contingent, as opposed to the necessary existence of *Atzmut*.

It is precisely in and by way of the *Or Ein Sof*—through the process of *tzimtzum*—that creation takes place[43] (as will be discussed below). In this way, the entire process of creation causes no change within God Himself, for *Atzmut* and the *Or Ein Sof* are not consubstantial.

We are still left with one problem: If God withdrew Himself from the void by way of the *tzimtzum*, the creation that exists within the void is devoid of God's Essence—*Atzmut*. Although this takes care of the problem of pantheism, for reasons that we will discuss in chapter 6, this position is untenable. Rabbi Shneur Zalman of Liadi therefore adopts the idea of *tzimtzum* proposed by the *Arizal*, adding some important qualifications. First, he declares, the *tzimtzum* is not to be understood literally,[44] that God actually withdrew Himself from the void. Nor did He withdraw the *Or Ein Sof*. Rather, God merely concealed the *Or Ein Sof*, by raising it up to a level beyond revelation,[45] analogous to the

---

inappropriate as an analogy for the *Ma'or* and the *Or Ein Sof*. See *Mishnat Chabad—Sefer HaArachim HaKatzar, Or Ein Sof*, chap. 4.

40. *Sefer HaArachim*, vol. 3, p. 64ff; pp. 73ff.

41. *Sefer HaMa'amarim 5656*, pp. 16, 432, 465.

42. See *Mishnat Chabad—Sefer HaArachim HaKatzar, Or Ein Sof*, chap. 3, for the sources.

43. *Sefer HaMa'amarim 5666*, pp. 166ff; *Derech Mitzevotecha*, p. 130aff.

44. As several kabbalists maintained. Their views will be presented in chapter 6.

45. *Shaar HaYichud v'HaEmunah*, chap. 7; *Likkutei Torah Vayikra*, ad loc.

invisibility of light waves higher in the spectrum than blue, or the
inaudibility of sound waves that are of a higher pitch than that
which can be heard by the human ear. Moreover, since the
tzimtzum took place only in the *Or Ein Sof*, and not in God
Himself, no change whatsoever is effected in Him by the
tzimtzum, and the principle of God's immutability is thus upheld.[46] God remains exactly as He was prior to the creation.

It must be noted again that the *Or Ein Sof* is not *Atzmut*, even
though it is "like the Luminary" and cleaves to it. Furthermore, it
does not even reveal *Atzmut*. That is, not only do we not know the
nature of *Atzmut* from the *Or Ein Sof*, we cannot even know of the
existence of *Atzmut* from *Or Ein Sof*. The reason for this is as
follows: The *Or Ein Sof* reveals only that which is relevant to it,
and since the main aspect of *Atzmut* is not that the *Or Ein Sof*
issues forth from Him, it is not possible that we can know
Atzmut from it.[47] In this sense, the relationship between
Atzmut and the *Or Ein Sof* is not the same as that between
the sun and the rays of the sun. In the latter case, the essence of
the sun is that it gives forth light, for this is the purpose for which
it was created, as is stated explicitly in the verse, "God set them
[the sun and moon] in the firmament of the heaven to give light
upon the earth" (Genesis 1:17). This is not so as regards
Atzmut—"it is not His entire Essence that the *Or Ein Sof* issues
forth from Him."[48] Nevertheless, this does not mean to say that
the *Or Ein Sof* reveals nothing whatsoever. Rather, it reveals only
those aspects of *Atzmut* that can be revealed by the *Or Ein
Sof*—that is not all of *Atzmut*, nor even the main aspects
thereof.[49]

In what way, then, can *Atzmut* be known, if not by way of the

---

46. *Tanya*, chap. 20; *Shaar HaYichud v'HaEmunah*, chap. 7.
47. *Sefer HaArachim*, vol. 3, p. 82.
48. Ibid., vol. 3, p. 78.
49. Ibid., vol. 3, p. 90.

Or Ein Sof? Through creation.[50] The reason that created being is able to reveal *Atzmut* is because "He alone has it in His power and ability to create something out of absolute naught and nothingness,[51] without this 'something' having any other cause preceding it." That is, creation is through the power of *Atzmut*,[52] for only He whose existence is of His Essence, and is not caused by some other cause preceding Himself, is able to bring into existence from absolutely nothing.[53] Accordingly, from the physical existence that we see, we know of the existence of *Atzmut*.[54]

The ramifications of this doctrine are far-reaching, having special bearing on the purpose of creation and the descent of the soul in the view of the chasidic masters, as will be discussed in the next chapter.

---

50. See *Sefer HaMa'amarim 5666*, p. 464.

51. That only God has the power to create *ex nihilo* is also expressed in the first of Maimonides' Thirteen Principles of Faith: "I believe with complete faith that the Creator, Blessed is His Name, creates and directs all created beings, and that He alone made, makes, and will make everything (Maimonides, *Commentary to the Mishnah, Sanhedrin*, chap. 11). The First Principle involves belief in the existence of God, that He is the Primary Existence, and that all of existence derives only from His true existence, existing only by virtue of the reality of His existence (see *Code, Foundations of the Torah* 1:1). That Maimonides' intention is precisely this is explained in many places by the Lubavitcher Rebbe, among them in a discourse entitled *Anochi Hashem Elokecha 5749* (1989), chap. 3.

52. *Tanya, Iggeret HaKodesh*, chap. 20, p. 130b; *Biurei HaZohar* (R. Dov Ber), p. 43c; *Derech Mitzevotecha*, p. 128bff.

53. Ibid.

54. *Yechaiyenu 5694*, chap. 14.

6

The Purpose of Creation and the Descent of the Soul—as relates to the *Zohar*, the *Arizal*, and Chasidism

In the previous chapter, we emphasized the distinction between *Atzmut* ("the Essence of God") and *Or Ein Sof* ("the Infinite Light"). It was pointed out that according to chasidic teachings in general, and *Chabad* teachings in particular, the *Or Ein Sof* does not reveal *Atzmut*, whereas the creation of the material world does, since "He alone has it in His power and ability to create something out of absolute naught and nothingness, for only He whose existence is of His Essence, and is not caused by some other cause preceding Himself, is able to create *ex nihilo*." This can be understood further by examining the various reasons that have been given for the purpose of creation.

For centuries, philosophers and theologians have toiled to understand God's purpose in creating the world. The physical world, limited in time and space, issued forth in some mysterious way from God's absolute Oneness and transcendent infinity. Leaving aside for the moment the question of how a world of finitude and multiplicity was created from God's oneness and infinity, a subject we will discuss in chapters 7 and 8, we must ask: What was God's purpose in creating such a world?

Kabbalistic sources offers several answers to this question. These answers may be grouped into two basic approaches:

The *Zohar*[1] answers that God created the world so that the creation will strive to know Him, or, more specifically, to know Him by way of each of His attributes.[2] The word for "world" in Hebrew is *olam*, a derivative of the word *he'elem* meaning "concealment," for the process of creation and the development of various planes of existence (called the various "worlds" in *Kabbalah*)[3] comes about by progressive levels of God's self-concealment (as will be explained below). Accordingly, each successive "world" is a lesser plane of Divine revelation. Any world, even the very highest of them (i.e., where Godliness is most revealed) is, by definition, a limitation of some sort or another, for the infinity and transcendence of God must be

---

1. Vol. 2, p. 42a.

2. Ibid., p. 42b.

3. There are five "worlds" spoken about in *Kabbalah*. The higher the world, the greater the revelation of God's Infinite Light (the *Or Ein Sof*). The lower the world, the less the revelation. Our material world is the lowest level of the lowest plane of existence.

concealed to some extent in order for that plane of existence to come into being. The lower the world, the more concealed Godliness is in that world, until in this world, Godliness is so concealed that one might even come to the conclusion that there is no God at all, or that even if God exists, the only existence one can prove is one's own (solipsism). Of course, from the Jewish point of view, the opposite is true:[4] The only real (i.e., completely independent) existence is God's, and all other existence is dependent upon His existence.[5] For this reason, God's existence is called necessary existence, whereas all the rest of existence is known as contingent existence,[6] as discussed in the previous chapter. The "mission" of all creation is to strive to know God—that is, to realize that all of creation and existence is only from God, and that all of creation is totally and constantly dependent upon Him for its very existence.

R. Yitzchak Luria, the *Arizal*, offers a second solution[7] to this question: Since it is axiomatic that God is perfect and complete in every way, had He not manifested his powers on the physical plane as well, we would not have called Him complete. If we say that God's power is manifested on infinite planes of existence but not on finite planes of existence, we detract from His perfection and completeness.[8] Therefore, in order to reveal that He is not limited to infinite revelation, He also created a finite world.

A variation of this explanation[9] is that God is the essence of kindness on every possible level, and it arose in His will to create the world as an expression of that kindness, "for He desires

---

4. Maimonides, *Code: Yesodei HaTorah*, chap. 1
5. Maimonides, *Code: Yesodei HaTorah*, chap. 1.
6. See *Pirush* to *Code*, ad loc.
7. Beginning of *Eitz Chaim; Sha'ar HaHakdamot, Hakdamah* 3.
8. Rabbi Meir ibn Gabbai in *Avodat HaKodesh* 1:8.
9. *Eitz Chaim; Sha'ar HaHakdamot*, chap. 3.

kindness,"[10] as it is written, "I want kindness, not sacrifices" (Hosea 6:6), and "it is the nature of the Good One to do good." Accordingly, if there was no world, to whom could He do good?[11] Thus, He created several planes of existence, including this physical world with all the different kinds of creatures that inhabit it, in order to express His kindness on every level of existence, from the very highest to the very lowest. The answer to the question of why God created the world, therefore is, that God created this physical world so that He could express His kindness toward even the very lowest and most undeserving level of existence.

CHASIDISM ON CREATION

Chasidic thought, based on a midrashic source,[12] offers a different answer to the mystery of creation. God created the world because "He desired to have a home [or dwelling place] in the lower worlds." Before we explain exactly what this means, it should be pointed out that this view invalidates the question as to why God created the world.

The question as to why the world was created must be understood in its proper perspective. When a human being performs an action, there is a motive, conscious or subconscious, that leads to the act itself. Moreover, this is the necessary order in which they occur—motive followed by action. A person's motive is thus the reason for, and cause of, his action. However, the same rule of motive and action does not apply to the Creator. When He does something, it is not because He first has a reason for doing

---

10. Michah 7:18.
11. See *Emek HaMelech, Sha'ar Sha'ashuei HaMelech*, chap. 1.
12. *Midrash Tanchuma, Nasso*, para. 16, cited in *Tanya*, chap. 36.

so and then acts accordingly. For "reason" is also a created entity. As far as God is concerned, His "reason" for doing something is merely an explanation that follows His actions, rather than preceding them. First He wills something, and then He creates the reason.

An analogy can be given. Parents love their child. When asked why they love their child, they might say, "Because my child is smart or cuddly or adorable . . ." However, it is self-evident that parents' love for their children is not based on anything special the child has or does not have, does or does not do, but because the child came from the parent's essence. It is a natural, innate love that may even defy all logic and reason, because the love comes before the reason that justifies it. The reason is true, but it is not what the love is based on. It is based on something beyond reason.

So, too, when God wills something, such as the creation of the world, His will is not the product of reason. On the contrary, reason is the product of His will. Consequently, the question as to why God created the world is invalid. He created it because He wanted to create it. Any reason that may be given for the creation follows, rather than precedes, the actual creation. Rabbi Shneur Zalman of Liadi expressed it this way: "Regarding a desire ('God desired to create the world,' in the words of the *Midrash*), one cannot ask questions."[13]

That is, God's motive for creating this world is His will or desire—which transcends reason. In technical kabbalistic terms, will or desire corresponds to the loftiest of all the *sefirot* ("divine attributes" or "emanations")—*keter*,[14] whereas reason corresponds to *chochmah binah*. The former is a transcendent, all-encompassing *sefirah*, which is inaccessible to human understanding, whereas the latter is the highest immanent and individualized attribute and is therefore accessible to human knowledge.

---

13. Cited in *Torah Or, Balak*, p. 997.
14. See *Pardes, Sha'ar Arachei HaKinuim*, s.v.

Thus, we cannot know why God created the world, according to the *Midrash*. Nevertheless, we can know what His purpose was in creating the world, in other words, what it was that He wanted when He created this world[15]—a "home" for Himself.

But what exactly is meant by the statement, "God desired a home in the lower worlds?" This concept comprises two main features:[16]

1. This world is a permanent[17] home for the Essence of God (*Atzmut*),[18] although not for the various levels of revelation that correspond to the various levels of *Or Ein Sof*.[19] On the contrary, *Or Ein Sof* is revealed in the higher worlds, not in the lowest world. By way of analogy in regard to man:[20] One of the most important features of a person's home is that this is where he feels most comfortable and most at ease—"at home." He does not have to play any roles or wear his garments of office. He can simply be himself. The intention of the *Midrash*, therefore, is that God wanted to be Himself as He is in His Essence down here in this world, transcending the levels of Godliness that are revealed in the various higher worlds. This is brought about by the fulfillment of the commandments in this world.[21]

2. *Atzmut* is revealed in this world.[22] This comes about

---

15. *Likkutei Sichot*, vol. 14, p. 123; vol. 15, p. 248; *Sefer HaLikkutim*, s.v., chap. 1.

16. *Likkutei Sichot*, vol. 4, p. 1054; vol. 3, p. 956, n. 11.

17. *Sefer HaMa'amarim 5666*, pp. 169ff, 432ff; *Likkutei Sichot*, vol. 16, p. 140.

18. See also *Or HaTorah Balak*, p. 997; *Sefer HaMa'amarim 5666*, p. 3; *Likkutei Sichot*, vol. 6, p. 22, n. 71, 77.

19. *Likkutei Sichot*, vol. 16, p. 140.

20. See *Machshevet HaChassidut*, R. Yoel Kahan, p. 10.

21. *Likkutei Sichot*, vol. 3, p. 956, n. 11.

22. See *Mishnat Chabad*, *Dirah Betachtonim*, chap. 3, para. 2.

through the love and awe with which a person fulfills the commandments.[23] To continue with the previous analogy:[24] If a person's home is dark and dingy, despite the fact that this is where he does not have to play any roles but can simply be himself, it can hardly be called a home worthy of the name.

Accordingly, when the *Midrash* talks of "God's desire for a home in the lowest world," it means two things: (1) that this is a place where God is as He is in Himself and; (2) that nothing obscures this fact—in other words, the fact that the world has been transformed into His "home" must be openly revealed to all.

Chasidic texts explain that God's desire in creating the world will find its fulfillment in the messianic era and, especially, in the time of the Resurrection of the Dead. At that time, "Your Teacher shall no longer hide Himself" (Isaiah 30:20). That is, not only will this world become the place "where God can be Himself, at home," this will also be revealed to everyone without any obstruction or concealment—"your eyes shall see your Teacher"—so that "the glory of the Lord shall be revealed and all flesh (even the physical flesh) shall see together" (Isaiah 40:5).

This idyllic situation—the "culminating fulfillment of the messianic era and the Resurrection of the Dead"—nevertheless "depends on our actions and service throughout the duration of the exile"[25] in which the Jewish people presently find themselves. That is, through the fulfillment of Torah and *mitzvahs*, which are the expression of God's innermost will[26] and in which He has invested His Essence,[27] this world is made into a "home" for God.

---

23. Ibid., para. 5.
24. *Machshevet HaChassidut*, ad loc.
25. *Tanya* chap. 37 p. 46b.
26. *Tanya*, chap. 36 p. 46a.
27. As the Talmud (*Shabbat* 105a) states regarding the Torah: "I gave

Accordingly, when a Jew learns Torah and fulfills *mitzvahs*,
whether he does this with love and awe, or whether he does it
without any emotional arousal, or even if he does it for some
other reason (*shelo lishmah*), the fulfillment itself nevertheless
draws down the Essence of God into this world.

However, if one learns Torah and fulfills *mitzvahs* without love
and awe, although a "home" is made for God, it is nevertheless a
dark and dingy abode. That is, the Essence of God is not revealed
thereby. Furthermore, if this was done for the wrong reasons
(*shelo lishmah*), not only is God not revealed, His presence is
actually obscured. For this reason, it is important to learn Torah
and fulfill the commandments with love and awe—so that God's
abode will be illuminated by them.[28]

Of course, this does not mean that the fulfillment of Torah and
mitzvahs, and the love and awe with which they are fulfilled, are
on a par. The actual fulfillment of God's will is primary, as ruled
in the Talmud[29] and the Codes,[30] so that if one had all the
intentions described in *Kabbalah* but did not do the actual deed,
nothing was achieved.[31]

Thus, chasidic philosophy declares that the status of this world
is not in any way lesser than the status of the higher worlds. On
the contrary: "Clearly, the purpose of the devolution [*hishtalshelut*]
of the worlds[32] and their descent, degree by degree, is not for the
sake of the higher worlds, because for them this is a descent from

---

Myself in writing"—(*Likkutei Torah Shelach* 48dff. See also *Tanya*, chap.
47.

28. See *Tanya*, chap. 38, at length.
29. *Berachot* 20b.
30. *Shulchan Aruch, Orach Chaim* 62:3.
31. See *Tanya*, chap. 38, at length.
32. This is the opposite of evolution. Evolutionary theory posits an
ascent and development from lower and simpler life forms to higher and
more complicated ones. *Kabbalah* explains that the opposite is true—the
worlds descend from a higher and greater revelation of Godliness to a

the light of His blessed Countenance. But the ultimate purpose [of creation] is this lowest world . . ."[33]

As we explained previously, the lower the world, the less the revelation of Godliness therein. The purpose of the entire process of devolution of the worlds is the material world, the one in which we live, for it was God's will (or "desire" in the language of the *Midrash*) that His Essence be revealed ("at home") precisely in the place where His "light"—the *Or Ein Sof*—is least revealed.[34] Moreover, this was His original intention, as in the expression[35] "the final deed arose first in thought."

This needs some further explanation: Whereas the existence of the higher worlds may be understood as an expression of God's revelation of His attribute of kindness and His perfection and completeness, and the objective of the creation is to strive to know Him, this cannot be the purpose of the creation of the lower worlds, in which He is not known and which do not reveal His attributes. The sole basis of the creation of this lowly world, therefore, is His desire to create it!

Whereas the higher worlds achieve the (secondary) purpose of revealing His attributes, this is not true of the lowest world. Moreover, in the higher worlds, this secondary purpose tends to conceal the fact that the entire process of creation is ultimately because of the pure desire of God to create it. However, since this world has no other merit (in the sense of revelation of Godliness) than the fact that God desired to create it, this is precisely what is revealed in this world and in no other—God's desire to create this world and dwell in it. This grants an infinite importance to this physical world, for it is God's "home."

---

lesser and lower revelation of Godliness. Therefore, this process may be dubbed "devolution."

33. *Tanya*, chap. 36, p. 45b.
34. *Tanya*, chap. 36–37.
35. Recited in the Friday night liturgy in the hymn called *Lecha Dodi*.

From this point of view, we can understand the limitations of the first answer cited as to why God created the worlds—so that "the creation will strive to know Him, or to know Him by way of each of His attributes." First, it is abundantly clear that man can never understand the Essence of God, for "no thought can grasp You at all."[36] Human intellect is unable to fathom even God's reasons for doing things ("regarding God's desires, one cannot ask questions"), let alone understand His very Essence. As far as understanding the creation of the world,[37] even King Solomon, the wisest of men, said, "However wise I will be, it is still far from me" (*Kohelet* 7:23). Accordingly, to know God cannot be the ultimate purpose of creation. Second, what can be known about God is far more accessible in the higher worlds than in this world, since the loftier the world, the more the *Or Ein Sof* is revealed in it, as explained above. Hence, the knowledge of God cannot be the ultimate purpose of this world wherein Godliness is hidden to the greatest degree.[38]

Regarding the explanation of the *Arizal*, cited above—had He not manifested His powers on the physical plane as well, we would not have called Him complete—it is pointed out[39] that this cannot be the ultimate reason for the creation of this world either. God was complete and perfect before any of the worlds were created. Only in the created worlds are potential and actual two different things, so that something that is in a state of potential is lacking actuality. But Above, this is not the case—as soon as it arose in His will to create, the worlds were created immediately.[40] Thus, there was no need to create this lowly world

---

36. *Tikkunei Zohar*, Introduction, p. 17a–b.

37. See Rashi's commentary to this verse.

38. *Sefer HaMa'amarim 5666*, pp. 5–7; *Sefer HaMa'amarim 5702*, chap. 18.

39. Ibid.

40. See *Pardes Sha'ar HaTzachtzachot*, chap. 3.

in order to achieve the revelation of His completeness and perfection.

This does not mean that the reasons given by the *Zohar* and the *Arizal* are incorrect. They are true explanations of how the Essence of God is revealed in the world (how God's home may be "illuminated" through learning Torah and fulfilling *mitzvahs* with love and awe). But the actual making of a home for God's Essence is dependent on fulfilling Torah and *mitzvahs*, not on the way in which they are fulfilled.

One of the major differences between the views expressed in *Kabbalah* and those expressed in the *Midrash*, cited in chasidic texts, can be understood by way of the following imaginary argument: If the creation was the result of some reason that God had for creating it (one of the two reasons cited above, or any other possible reason), then the creation itself has importance in its own right, for it fulfills the Creator's purpose! Accordingly, man is of utmost importance to God, for he is the one entrusted with making this world God's home in actuality (as will be explained shortly). Therefore, the more a particular person understands his Creator, or the more he reflects God's attributes, the more important he will be to God, and consequently to all of creation, for God needs him to fulfill his purpose in creating the world! Of course, such a conclusion is absurd and is not much better than the philosophy of solipsism mentioned above.

According to chasidic thought, however, there was no reason for the creation. God did not need it; He only desired it. Accordingly, the creation itself has no intrinsic value or importance, and God does not need man in order to fulfill whatever reason He had for creating the world. It follows that in order to invite God into the "home" that He created for Himself, a person must nullify his own existence,[41] as the Sages state regarding an

---

41. *Likkutei Sichot*, vol. 5, p. 21, n. 70; *Sefer HaMa'amarim 5661*.

arrogant person, "I and he cannot dwell together,"[42] says God. Herein lies the entire concept of *bittul*, a central feature of chasidic thought.

FREE CHOICE

One of the main ideas in this concept of "making a home in the lower worlds for God's *Atzmut*," is that this should be achieved through the efforts and free choice of this world's inhabitants. True, God could certainly have made the world a place that naturally reveals His Essence, without any difficulty or opposition. However, that is not what He wanted. He wanted us to make this world a home for Him. With man's own efforts and choice, he can refine and purify the world so that it will become a home for God, instead of Him having to force His way in: "This culminating fulfillment of the messianic era and of the Resurrection of the Dead . . . depends on our actions and service throughout the duration of the exile."[43] After all, a home is where one can feel most comfortable. When one forces oneself into another person's home, one does not feel at ease or comfortable. If the world does not prepare itself by its own efforts and this must instead be achieved through God's intervention and force, the ultimate goal has not been achieved.

The Talmud[44] relates that when God gave the Torah to the Jewish people, He suspended Mount Sinai over them, declaring that if they accepted the Torah, well and good, but if not, He would drop the mountain on them. The Talmud goes on to explain that this is a classical case of an agreement obtained under

---

42. *Arachin* 15b.

43. *Tanya*, chap. 37. See *Mishnat Chabad, Dirah Betachtonim*, chap. 3.

44. *Shabbat* 88a.

duress, which is not binding in Jewish law. Only later on, in the days of Mordechai and Esther, did they receive the Torah willingly, resulting in the dramatic story of Purim.[45]

This doctrine appears in many forms in chasidic thought. In chapter 2, we cited the teaching of the Maggid of Mezritch on the verse, "I made the earth and I created man upon it" (Isaiah 45:12):

> He who is the true "I," unknown to and concealed from even the loftiest emanations, clothed His Essence within numerous condensations to give rise to emanations and creatures, the various categories of angels, and worlds without number. Through countless condensations, "I made the earth and I created man upon it." Man is the purpose of creation, and *barati* [the Hebrew for "I created"], having the numerical equivalent[46] of 613 [the number of biblical commandments], is the purpose of man. . . ."

The importance of the material world and the actual performance of the commandments is further emphasized in a series of essays[47] written by the sixth Lubavitcher Rebbe, Rabbi J. I. Schneersohn, explaining the verse, "I have come into My garden, My sister, My bride" (Song of Songs 5:1). The Midrash[48] explains that the entire Song of Songs is to be understood as a metaphor

---

45. This interpretation is given in *Torah Or*, p. 96c.

46. Each letter of the Hebrew alphabet has a numerical equivalent, called *gematria*. Computation of *gematrias* is a well-known kabbalistic device for revealing mystical allusions of words and their connection to other words or events.

47. The series of discourses entitled *Basi LeGani 5710*, spanning twenty chapters, was written by Rabbi J. I Schneersohn shortly before he passed on. It was regarded by his son-in-law, Rabbi M. M. Schneerson, who became the seventh Lubavitcher Rebbe, as the spiritual legacy that his predecessor had left for the generation. Each year, for more than forty years, on the *yahrzeit* of Rabbi J. I. Sshneersohn's passing, the Rebbe elucidated one of the chapters of this discourse.

48. *Shir HaShirim Rabbah*.

for the relationship between God and His "bride"—the Jewish people. This verse is interpreted by the *Midrash* as referring to the Sanctuary in the desert, in which the Divine Presence [the *Shechinah*] was revealed. The *Midrash* continues, explaining that in the beginning, the essence of the *Shechinah* was revealed in this lowly world. However, in the wake of the sin of the Tree of Knowledge, the *Shechinah* departed from the earth and rose into the heavens. Later on, through the sins of one generation after the other (for six more generations), the *Shechinah* withdrew further and further from this world. Subsequently, through the devoutness of seven generations of righteous *tzaddikim*, starting with Abraham, Isaac, and Jacob, the *Shechinah* was drawn down again, from level to level, until Moses, the seventh of these *tzaddikim*, drew the revelation of the *Shechinah* down once again into this world below, for:

> The ultimate purpose for the creation of the [physical and spiritual] worlds was that "God desired to have a home in the lower worlds." He desired that Divinity be revealed below—by means of man's Divine service of subordinating and transforming his physical nature.[49] He desired that the divine soul descend from its spiritual heights and become clothed in a body with an animal soul . . . [so that] the divine soul would refine and purify the body and the animal soul, as well as its portion in the world, that is, its environment.[50]

The essay explains further that when this process of transformation and refinement is complete, then the essence of the *Shechinah* will be revealed in this material world once again. The seventh Lubavitcher Rebbe, Rabbi M. M. Schneerson, explains that when the *Midrash* (and his predecessor, the sixth Lubavitcher Rebbe)

---

49. See, at length, chapter 3.
50. *Basi LeGani 5710*, chap. 1.

used the expression "the essence of the *Shechinah*" they meant "the essential and innermost degree of *Shechinah*."[51] He writes:

> The [Divine] illumination clothed within the world descends in an orderly and progressive manner, so that the loftier the world, the greater the degree of illumination; the lower the world within the progressive chain of descent [of the worlds], the lesser the illumination. This is generally so regarding the illumination found within progressively descending levels. [Accordingly, there is a greater degree of revelation in the higher worlds than in the lower worlds, as is explained above]. Although it is true that before the sin [of the Tree of Knowledge] the illumination was revealed in this world as well, nevertheless, even then the illumination was revealed to a greater extent in the higher worlds. . . . We must therefore say that the above statement [that the essence of the *Shechinah* was originally found in this lowly world] refers to the illumination that transcends all worlds; this is what is meant by the essence of the *Shechinah*.

Chapters 9 and 10 of the same essay[52] go on to clarify that this is all actualized by the actual fulfillment of the commandments. God did not leave it to us to choose or discover our own means and methods of making this world His home. Rather, He provided us with all the necessary tools—the Torah and its 613 commandments (*mitzvahs*). God's commandments are His will. He commanded us to take a physical object and to carry out His will through that object.

Almost every *mitzvah* deals with a physical object. By carrying out that commandment, a person's connection through the physical action and with a physical object is with God Himself.[53]

---

51. *Basi LeGani 5711*, chap. 1.

52. Elucidated by the discourses of the seventh Rebbe on these chapters—*Basi LeGani 5719*, chaps. 5ff; *Basi LeGani 5720*, chaps. 4ff; *Basi LeGani 5739*.

53. Explained at length in *Tanya*, chap. 35.

For example, when a woman lights candles prior to the onset of the Sabbath, she recites the blessing "He sanctified us with His commandment and commanded us to light the Sabbath candles." By fulfilling the commandment, she binds herself to God. In fact, the word *mitzvah* ("commandment") stems from the word *tzavta*, meaning "connection" or "attachment."[54] Thus, the candle she lights becomes a "home" for God, for this is where His will is carried out. Each *mitzvah* deals with another part of the physical world. By observing the commandments, every person makes his part of the world a home for God, and so, collectively, we are all occupied with making the world a dwelling place for Him. Moreover, when we use a physical object in the performance of a *mitzvah*, we transform the physical object into a vehicle for holiness. In this sense, a person's deeds build a "home" for God within this material world.

Moreover, in no other world is there access to God's will in the same way, for in no world, other than this one, did God demand that the world make Him a home. The inhabitants of all the other worlds (angels and all types of spiritual manifestations and attributes) merely bask in God's glory. True, the angels sing God's praises, but this is their natural response. They are neither required to do so, nor is it against their nature. The only place that God actually asked that His will be fulfilled is in this world. Therefore, only in this world is there access to the Essence of God—through His commandments.

To take this a step further: The idea of God's desire to dwell in the lower world is appreciated even more in the mundane experiences of everyday life, such as when one is eating, sleeping, or working. Even while we fulfill tasks that are necessary for our continued physical existence (tasks that have no overt spiritual content) we have the possibility, rather, the obligation, of sanctifying

---

54. *Torah Or*, p. 82a; *VeKibel HaYehudim* in *Sefer HaMa'amarim 5687*, p. 110.

them, as the verse states, "Know Him in all your ways" (*Mishlei* 3:6)—in all your ways, that is, those that are defined as yours, and not those that God has commanded you to do. Similarly, by looking for Divine providence in worldly events, a person sanctifies the events themselves.This perhaps is one of the reasons that in his teachings, the Ba'al Shem Tov discussed how we should go about our daily lives when we are not directly involved in Torah and *mitzvahs.* Chasidism did not come to add any more commandments to the 613. Rather, it emphasizes that serving God is a 24-hour-a-day, 365-day-a-year job. There is not a single moment that is left open or optional, and no area that is ultimately outside of the realm of holiness. Even the lowest and most trivial experience or object can become a vehicle for Godliness.

Let us once again cite the letter from the seventh Lubavitcher Rebbe, written to the organizers of the International Seminar on Jewish Mysticism, which we quoted at the beginning of this study. It provides a clear summary of the chasidic position:

> Jewish mysticism teaches that the purpose of the soul's descent to earth is to reveal the harmony that is inherent in the created world, beginning with the "small world," namely, man—a creature of *nigleh* ["revealed aspects"] and *nistar* ["hidden aspects"], of a body and a soul. Inner personal peace and harmony can be achieved only through the supremacy of the soul over the body, since, in the nature and scheme of things, the body can be made to submit to the soul—willingly, and in the case of the true mystic, even eagerly—but not vice versa.
>
> Jewish mysticism helps to realize the said purpose of the soul by teaching it how to recognize the spirituality of matter, and that in every physical thing, even in the inanimate, there is a "soul," which is the creative force that has created it—a being out of non-being—and continuously keeps from reverting back to its former state of nonexistence. It is this "spark" of Godliness that is the true essence and reality of all things, and this spark is released and revealed when physical matter is used for a sublime purpose

or deed in accordance with the Will of the Creator, as for example, in the performance of a *mitzvah*. . . .

One of the aspects of *Chabad* is to reveal and expound the esoteric aspects of the Torah and *mitzvahs* so that they can be comprehended by the three intellectual faculties—*chochmah, binah, da'at*—and reduced to rational categories, down to the actual performance of the *mitzvahs*, showing how, in the final analysis, God can be "comprehended" better by action (the performance of the *mitzvahs*) than by meditation, which is one of the cardinal differences between Jewish and non-Jewish mysticism. . . .

In light of the above, the physical world in which we live must be viewed through far more optimistic lenses than is commonly done in the mystical milieu. True, this material world is at a disadvantage in that it lacks the quantity and quality of *Or Ein Sof*, which illuminates the other worlds to a greater or lesser degree. Its advantage, however, is that through the fulfillment of Torah and *mitzvahs* in this world, and in this world only, God's Essence is accessible.

Furthermore, the ultimate fulfillment of a Jew's spiritual mission is not for him to transcend his physical limitations as his soul soars aloft in contemplation of the higher planes of reality, copiously illuminated by the *Or Ein Sof*. Rather, the ultimate purpose of man's existence is achieved as a soul clothed within a body as he fulfills the commandments of his Creator in this world, for this, and only this, "comprehends" God's Essence.

A story told by the *Tzemach Tzedek*, the illustrious grandson of Rabbi Shneur Zalman, and his eventual successor, illustrates this idea: On several occasions he heard his grandfather declare in a state of Godly rapture, "I do not wish to see anything. I do not want Your *Gan Eden* [Paradise]. I do not want Your World to Come . . . I want nothing more than You alone!"[55]

---

55. In *Derech Mitzevotecha*, p. 138a (close to the end of the page).

7

THE PROCESS OF CREATION: *T*ZIMTZUM AND RELATED CONCEPTS

In chapter 5 we examined the question of how Jewish thinkers reconciled the ineffable *Atzmut* with the finite universe, the Oneness of God and the existence of multiplicity, and so on. Among the solutions that they offered are those called "intermediate agency" and "emanationism"—in other words, that creation came into being by way of a series of intermediate steps, emanated by the Creator, that place a sufficiently great distance between Him and that which He created, so that the corporeality and the multiplicity of the latter are disassociated and set apart from God Himself. In other words, the creation came about by way of a long chain of evolutionary processes, a chain of cause and effect, emanated by the Creator as the First (and very distant)

Cause, until eventually the corporeality of this material world came into being.

We also cited the view of R. Moshe Cordovero[1] (*Ramak*)—that in order to avoid the implication of a direct continuity between the Creator and the created (the classical pantheistic view) there must be a series of intermediate steps—according to his view, these are the ten *sefirot*, including *keter*, which are produced by the Creator and which provide a gradual descent from the transcendent infinity of *Atzmut* to the plane of immanent, finite being. Each succeeding *sefirah* from *keter* downward represents a descending level of spirituality, a series of causes and effects wherein each successive level is emanated by the previous level, until the lowest of the *sefirot, malchut,* eventually evolves. The actual creation comes about only from the level of *malchut.* Thus, a sufficiently great distance has been placed between Him and that which He created. Corporeality and the multiplicity of creation is disassociated and set apart from God Himself.

However, we pointed out that *Ramak's* solution does not solve the problem, for the question as to how, and at what point, the changeover from infinite to finite takes place has not been answered: As long as there is some causal relationship between the Creator and the created, between the first link in the evolutionary chain and the last, no matter how long the chain might be, there always remains some association between one level and another, and thus between the first link and the last.[2] Accordingly, the aspect of infinity is never completely nullified. On the contrary, because each successive level emanates from or is produced by the previous level, it "inherits" the infinity of its predecessor, so that finite material matter could never have been

---

1. *Pardes, sha'ar* 3, chap. 1.

2. *Tanya,* chap. 48; *Tanya, Iggeret HaKodesh,* chap. 20; *Likkutei Torah, Devarim,* pp. 46c, 20d. See Shochat, *Mystical Concepts in Chasidism,* chap. 2.

created from infinite spiritual being, despite numerous causes and effects interposed between the Creator and the created. Of course, the ultimate result of this is that a unity of substance between the Creator and the created (a classical case of pantheism) is implied. This was the very problem that R. Moshe Cordovero tried to avoid.

THE *TZIMTZUM*

It was explained that Rabbi Isaac Luria, the *Arizal*, therefore expounded the doctrine of *tzimtzum*.[3] In the *Arizal's* view the process of creation was not an uninterrupted sequence of causes and effects, nor a gradual descent of emanations. Rather, the primary act of creation was to establish a "gap" between the Creator and the created, a "quantum leap" (*dilug*) that breaks the gradualism and establishes a radical distinction between the First Cause and all subsequent effects.[4] This radical break is called the *tzimtzum*. The doctrine of *tzimtzum* was expounded by the *Arizal* in the following way: Before the universe was created, there was only the Infinite One, whose infinity filled all of existence. Within this infinity, there was no place for finite existence. But when it arose in God's will to create finite worlds, He withdrew Himself from the place where the finite worlds would exist after the *tzimtzum* in order to create a void (*makom panui* or *chalal*) wherein finite reality could exist. Finite being then came about by means of a reintroduction of finite light into the void.[5]

Although the doctrine of *tzimtzum* places a sufficiently great

---

3. See the beginning of *Eitz Chaim, Otzrot Chaim, Mevoh Shearim*, etc.

4. See *Torah Or, Esther* 90a, 116c; *Likkutei Torah, Shir HaShirim* 40bff., 41d, 42bff. See Shochat, *Mystical Concepts in Chasidism*, chap. 2.

5. See the beginning of *Etz Chaim, Otzrot Chaim, Mevoh Shearim*, etc.;

distance between the Creator and the created, avoiding the problems of pantheism, it seems to place the wholly contingent created world entirely outside of God, as the classic theistic position maintains. In other words, if God withdrew Himself by way of the *tzimtzum*, leaving a *makom panui*, the creation that exists within the *makom panui* is devoid of God's—*Atzmut*. Moreover, this also implies a change within God, for prior to the creation He was everywhere and after the creation there is one place where He is not—the *makom panui*. This violates the basic principle that the creation does not bring about any change whatsoever in God—"I, God, have not changed" (Malachi 3:6).[6]

Rabbi Shneur Zalman of Liadi therefore adopts the idea of *tzimtzum* proposed by the *Arizal*, but adds some important qualifications regarding its interpretation. First, the *tzimtzum* is not to be understood literally,[7] that God actually withdrew Himself from the void. Nor did He withdraw the *Or Ein Sof*. Rather, God merely concealed the *Or Ein Sof*, by "raising it up" to a level beyond revelation,[8] much the same way as raising the pitch of audible sound makes it imperceptible to the human ear. Moreover, since the *tzimtzum* took place only in the *Or Ein Sof* and not in God Himself, no change whatsoever is affected in Him by the *tzimtzum*, and the principle of God's immutability is thus upheld.[9] God remains exactly as He was prior to the creation.

In order to explain the actual process of *tzimtzum*, as expressed in chasidic texts, a number of prefatory remarks must be made.

Tanya, chaps. 21, 48, 49; *Likkutei Torah Vayikra*, pp. 51bff., and especially 52c.

6. See the fourth of Maimonides' Thirteen Principles of Faith.

7. As several kabbalists maintained. Their views will be presented later.

8. *Shaar HaYichud v'HaEmunah*, chap. 7; *Likkutei Torah Vayikra*, ad loc.

9. *Tanya*, chap. 20; *Shaar HaYichud v'HaEmunah*, chap. 7.

LEVELS IN THE *OR EIN SOF*

The *Or Ein Sof* has an internal and an external aspect[10] (*pnimiut* and *chitzoniyut*). In a general sense, the *pnimiut* of the *Or Ein Sof* is called *etzem ha'or* ("the essence of the Infinite Light," not to be confused with *Atzmut*), whereas the *chitzoniyut* of the *Or Ein Sof* is called *hitpashtut ha'or* ("the diffusion or extension of the Infinite Light"). *Etzem ha'or* is the way the *Or Ein Sof* is within its source, the *Ma'or* ("Luminary"), whereas *hitpashtut ha'or* is the way the *Or Ein Sof* becomes extended and drawn downwards to become revealed.[11]

However, in a more specific way, three descending levels of *Or Ein Sof* are identified:

Etzem ha'Or "The essence of the light." This is the aspect of the *Or Ein Sof* that merges completely with its Source and is thus unidentifiable and set completely apart from the other levels of *Or Ein Sof* that emerge from it.

Ha'Or she'b'gilui l'Atzmo "The light that is revealed only to Himself." Its purpose is to reveal Godliness and bring about a state of total existential nullification, called *bittul b'metzius*[12] in chasidic terminology. This is also the source of the (post-*tzimtzum*) *Or HaSovev kol Almin*, the transcendent light that both envelops

---

10. This is due to the *ha'akava of Atzmut*, an act of "self-constraint" prior to the *tzimtzum*—in order to produce the *Or Ein Sof*, as explained in chapter 4. See *Torat Shalom*, p. 147; *Sichat Shabbat Parshat Tetzaveh 5745*, chap. 20–22; *Sefer HaMa'amarim 5662*, p. 322ff.

11. *Sefer HaMa'amarim 5666*, pp. 510–516. See, at length, *Mishnat Chabad—Sefer HaArachim Hakatzar Or Ein Sof*, chap. 5.

12. *Sefer HaMa'amarim 5672*, chap. 128ff; *Anochi Hashem Elokecha 5703*, chap. 3; *Shuva Yisrael 5705*, chap. 16; *Vayered Havaye al Har Sinai 5715*.

and pervades all of creation without ever being perceived by creation.[13]

Ha'Or hashayach l'olamot   "The light that is relevant to the worlds." This light suffuses each of the worlds and is revealed within each of them, according to the level of each world. This level is the source of the (post-*tzimtzum*) *Or HaMemalei kol Almin*, the immanent revelation of light that "fills all worlds" and permeates all created beings as their very existence and life-force.[14] In fact, to create and sustain the existence of all the worlds is precisely the purpose of the extension of this level of light. Nevertheless, even this level of light is far too sublime to give rise to material existence[15] without the *tzimtzum*.

Prior to the *tzimtzum*, this level of *Or Ein Sof* is described in the writings of the *Arizal*[16] as follows: "Initially everything was supernal, uncompounded light which filled all of existence . . . It had no beginning and no end, but was uniform in every way . . . When it rose in His will to create worlds . . . He contracted [*tzimtzem*] Himself in the middle of His light. . . ."

Chasidic texts explain[17] that because the *Or Ein Sof* "had no beginning and no end, but was uniform in every way, when it rose in His will to create worlds," God "measured out within Himself in potential what would exist in the future in actuality." Or, in other words, He "measured out" within Himself how He would

---

13. See *Tanya*, chap. 48.

14. *Sefer HaMa'amarim 5672*, chap. 128ff; *Anochi Hashem Elokecha 5703*, chap. 3; *Shuva Yisrael 5705*, chap. 16; *Vayered Havaye al Har Sinai 5715*.

15. *Sefer HaMa'amarim 5662*, p. 323–4; *Sefer HaArachim Chabad*, vol. 3, p. 158.

16. *Eitz Chaim, drush Iggulim veYosher, anaf 2; Otzrot Chaim*, beginning; *Sha'ar HaHakdamot, hakdamah 4*.

17. *Sefer HaMa'amarim 5666*, pp. 515–517; *Sefer HaMa'amarim 5672*.

bring about a finite existence—prior to actually doing so. This "measuring out" is called in the *Zohar*[18] *galif galifu b'tehiru ila'ah*—"He engraved letters [or, 'engravings'] in the Supernal Purity" (the *Or Ein Sof*).[19] These "letters" signify the structuring and formation of the Divine Will prior to the *tzimtzum*, although (prior to the *tzimtzum*) they cannot yet be regarded as the manifestation of His will. They are therefore called only "the potential for limitation." *Chabad* texts refer to these "letters" as the "letters of the *reshimu* ['traces or imprints'] prior to the *tzimtzum*."[20]

Prior to the *tzimtzum* however, these "letters" are flooded with *Or Ein Sof*, so that the attribute of limitation that they constitute is not actualized but remains a mere potential for limitation. It is only after the *tzimtzum* that these "letters" become the root of finite being. One of the functions of the *tzimtzum*, therefore, is to remove the *Or Ein Sof* that floods these letters, so that limitation and finitude can be actualized. From this point of view, the effect of the *tzimtzum* is to prevent the *Or Ein Sof* from illuminating these letters, so that after the *tzimtzum* the letters of the *reshimu* remain as the actualization of the "measuring out" of the Divine Will. According to some views, they are also known as the *esser sefirot ha-genuzot beMa'atzilan*—"the ten primordial *sefirot* that are concealed within He who brought them forth."[21]

---

18. Vol. 1, p. 15a.

19. See *Hallelu'* 5656, p. 371; *Sefer HaMa'amarim 5677*, p. 18; *Sefer HaMa'amarim 5666*, p. 5–6; *Sefer HaArachim Chabad*, vol. 3, p. 270.

20. *Likkutei Torah Behar*, p. 43c; ibid., *Vayikra, Hosafot*, p. 53b–c; *Or HaTorah Devarim*, pp. 924–925.

21. R. Moshe Cordovero, *Pardes Sha'ar Hatzachtzachot*, chaps. 3, 6. See *Or HaTorah Beshallach*, p. 484; *Sefer HaMa'amarim 5666*, p. 184ff; *Derech Mitzevotecha*, p. 153a.

THE PURPOSE OF THE *TZIMTZUM*

The *tzimtzum* thus achieves two goals:[22]

1. On the one hand, the *tzimtzum* reveals the "wholeness" or "completeness" (*shleimut*) of the Holy One, blessed is He[23]—that God is not limited to infinite revelation (i.e., the *Or Ein Sof*), but has the ability as well of finite revelation, or, the other side of the coin, the ability to limit His infinite revelation. As mentioned in Chapter 4, if we say that God's power is manifested on infinite planes of existence, but not on finite planes of existence, we detract from His perfection and completeness.[24]

2. On the other hand, paradoxically, the act of *tzimtzum* is, in fact, for the purpose of revelation and not for the purpose of the concealment that it initially brings about. This may be explained in two ways: Because of the *tzimtzum*, without which the worlds could not have been created, in the future (in the messianic era and particularly with the subsequent Resurrection of the Dead)[25] the level of *Or Ein Sof* that illuminated all of existence prior to the *tzimtzum* will again be revealed. The only difference is that prior to the *tzimtzum*, this infinite revelation did not allow the existence of finite being, whereas after the *tzimtzum*, as a result of the fulfillment of Torah and *mitzvahs* in this physical world in the interim, the level of *Or Ein Sof* that illuminated all of existence prior to the *tzimtzum* will be revealed within the world, which will

---

22. The following is based on *Mishnat Chabad Tzimtzum*, chap. 2.

23. This is probably the most common appellation of God found in *Chabad* texts.

24. Rabbi Meir ibn Gabbai in *Avodat HaKodesh* 1:8.

25. *Tanya*, chaps. 36–37.

nevertheless continue to exist as a finite world. Second, not only will the same level of *Or Ein Sof* that illuminated all of existence become revealed, but the inner dimension and essence of the *Or Ein Sof*, which was never before revealed, will become manifested within the material world.

This can be explained by way of an analogy: When a great sage mulls over some concept in his mind, he does not need to simplify the concept for himself, for he understands it perfectly. However, when he wishes to communicate the concept to a student, he is obligated to abridge his own understanding of the concept so that it will be comprehensible to his student. After all, one cannot explain calculus to first grade students. Nevertheless, the purpose of the abridgement is, in fact, revelation—the teacher's intention is to teach his student as much as the student is ready for, until eventually, with the passage of time, the student will be able to attain his teacher's knowledge. This idea is reflected in a statement of the Talmud: "One should always teach one's students in a concise manner."[26]

According to the latter explanation, the *tzimtzum* is essentially for the sake of creating "vessels" for the *Or Ein Sof*—in other words, that which can contain and give outward form and expression to what is essentially infinite *Or Ein Sof*. In this regard, R. Yitzchak Luria states: The *tzimtzum* and reduction of the light enables the formation and revelation of *keilim* ["vessels"],[27] and reveals the root of *din* ["restriction, limitation"].[28] Therefore, in other words: In order for the unlimited *Or Ein Sof* to also be "internalized," (i.e., revealed in an immanent way within creation, instead of only transcending it), the *tzimtzum* was necessary.

To sum up: Although the process of *tzimtzum* causes a reduction and concealment of the *Or Ein Sof*, nevertheless, this is

---

26. *Pesachim* 3b.
27. *Eitz Chaim, sha'ar* 71, *anaf* 3.
28. Ibid., *anaf* 52.

not its purpose. Rather, the purpose is to create a physical world
sans revelation of Godliness, so that man, through his activities in
Torah and *mitzvahs*, can transforms this world into a "home" for
the Holy One.

FOUR VIEWS OF THE *TZIMTZUM*

We mentioned previously that the doctrine of *tzimtzum* does
not appear at all in the writings of R. Moshe Cordovero. It was
first proposed by the *Arizal* in order to explain that the process of
creation was not an uninterrupted sequence of causes and effects
or a gradual descent of emanations. Rather, a radical distinction,
called the *tzimtzum*, was made between the First Cause and all
subsequent effects.

The doctrine of *tzimtzum*, however, was formulated very tersely
and was apparently never explained by the *Arizal* at great length.
Accordingly, it was open to differing interpretations and, in fact,
became one of the major bones of contention between chasidim
and their opponents, the *mitnagdim*.[29]

It should be pointed out that according to R. Moshe Cordovero,
there is no question that the *Or Ein Sof* pervades all worlds and,
at the same time, transcends them, and that "no place is devoid of
Him."[30] Moreover, as regards the omnipresence of God, Chasidism adopts R. Moshe Cordovero's view,[31] which, at face-value,

---

29. Cf. Rabbi Shneur Zalman of Liadi's remark regarding those who
interpreted the *tzimtzum* literally: ". . . it is possible to understand the
error of some, scholars in their own eyes, may God forgive them, who
erred and misinterpreted in their study of the writings of the *Arizal* . . .
and understood the doctrine of *tzimtzum* . . . literally."

30. *Tikkunei Zohar, tikkun* 57, p. 91b.

31. Letter from the Ba'al Shem Tov in *Ginzei Nistarot*, vol. 1, para. 55.
Although the authenticity of this document is doubted by historians

appears to contradict the doctrine of *tzimtzum* proposed by the *Arizal*. (The former view affirms the omnipresence of God, while the latter seems to imply that God withdrew His presence from the area called the *makom panui*). However, *Chabad* texts interpret the *Arizal's* doctrine of *tzimtzum* in a way that agrees entirely with R. Moshe Cordovero's view.[32]

In order to understand how this is so, we must examine the various interpretations of the doctrine of *tzimtzum*.

Differing interpretations of the *tzimtzum* center around a disagreement regarding two concepts:[33]

1. Whether the *tzimtzum* is to be interpreted literally (as actual withdrawal), or not;
2. Whether the *tzimtzum* took place in the Infinite Light (the *Or Ein Sof*) or in the Luminary (God, or what we referred to earlier as *Atzmut*). Thus, there are four possible interpretations:[34]

Tzimtzum is meant literally and takes place in Atzmut: This means that the Holy One, blessed is He, removed His *Atzmut* from the place that was to become the worlds, leaving a *makom panui* or *chalal* that is devoid of God's Essence.[35] God then oversees matters from above the void. This is the view of R.

(who reject the entire *Genizat Herson* from which this letter comes) there is no doubt that it is accepted as genuine by the Rebbes of *Chabad*. See *Hatamim*, p. 227a.

32. See *Mishnat Chabad*, *Tzimtzum*, chap. 4. The entire subject is examined there at length.

33. See the Lubavitcher Rebbe's *Likkutei Sichot*, vol. 15, p. 470.

34. Ibid.

35. According to this view, the *makom panui* is devoid of *Atzmut*. According to other views cited, it is devoid only of the *Or Ein Sof*. Rabbi Shneur Zalman's view is that it is merely devoid of the revelation of the *Or Ein Sof*.

Emmanuel Chai Riki,[36] adopted by R. Elijah of Vilna.[37] One of
the proofs adduced for this literal interpretation of the *tzimtzum* is
that if the *tzimtzum* was only metaphorical, God's *Atzmut* would
be found in unworthy places and lowly things. Accordingly, He
removed His Essence from the place where He created a finite
world in which impurity is found. Nevertheless, God's *hashgacha*
("providence, overseeing") fills the void that is created by the
withdrawal of His *Atzmut*. This is comparable to a king sitting in
his palace and gazing upon a garbage heap. The garbage remains
at a sufficient distance from him that he cannot be said to be
associated with it. Nevertheless, it is not removed completely
from his realm of authority, for he has jurisdiction over it from his
palace window. Analogously, God's Essence is removed from the
makom panui and is not affected by what goes on in this material
creation. Nevertheless, this world remains within the realm of His
authority and jurisdiction because He provides it with its life-
force—from a distance, of course. But His Essence is not present
in the lowly worlds at all.[38] As for the *Zohar's* statement that "no
place is devoid of Him"—this is interpreted as meaning that no
place is devoid of His *hashgacha*.[39] The chasidic response to this
interpretation of *hashgacha* will be discussed in chapter 10.

**Tzimtzum is meant literally, but takes place in the Or Ein
Sof, not in Atzmut:**   This is the view maintained by R. Yonatan
Eibeschutz.[40] He writes that had the *Arizal* stated explicitly that

---

36. In *Yosher Leivav, Bayit 1, cheder 1*, chaps. 12, 13; and *Mishnat
Hasidism*, beginning.

37. In the *Likkutim* that follow his commentary to the *Sifra d'Tzeniuta*,
s.v.

38. See *Yosher Leivav*, ad loc.

39. See *Sifra d'Tzeniuta, Likkutim*, ad loc.

40. In *Shem Olam* (Vienna, 5651), pp. 231ff.

the *tzimtzum* took place in Atzmut,[41] we would have been forced to understand it this way. However, the *Arizal* mentions only the words *Or Ein Sof*; "the aspect of severity [*din*];" *malchut*, and so forth—none of which are *Atzmut*. He cites[42] R. Yisrael Sarug and R. Menachem deFano, who point out that the entire matter of *tzimtzum* takes place in God's Will, not in His *Atzmut*. He discusses the matter at length and absolutely rejects the interpretation of *tzimtzum* as the withdrawal of *Atzmut*.

R. Y. Eibeschutz then continues with a discussion of whether the *tzimtzum* itself should be interpreted literally or allegorically. He writes:

> Were it not for the fact that the *Arizal* clearly implies that the *tzimtzum* means a literal withdrawal, I would have interpreted [the word *tzimtzum*] as a borrowed expression, meaning that God conceals His presence in that place where the worlds exist, so that His presence cannot be comprehended. However, anyone who examines the words of the *Arizal* will see that one cannot interpret them this way since he speaks about actual withdrawal . . .[43]

He therefore concludes that the *tzimtzum* is a literal withdrawal. However, it is the withdrawal of *Or Ein Sof*, not *Atzmut*, from the *makom panui*. Thus, the entire *tzimtzum* takes place only in the *Or Ein Sof*, not in *Atzmut*.

Tzimtzum is not meant literally, but takes place in *Atzmut*: This view is maintained by R. Chaim of Volozhin.[44] He writes: The word *tzimtzum* in this context does not mean "withdrawal" or removal from one place to another . . . [but] in this context it

---

41. He uses the expression *Sibah Rishonah* ("the First Cause") to denote *Atzmut*.
42. Ibid., pp. 231–232.
43. Ibid., p. 238.
44. *Nefesh HaChaim, sha'ar* 3, chap. 7.

means "concealment" and "veiling." The intention is that God's Essential Oneness, which fills all worlds absolutely equally, is what we call *tzimtzum*. This is because God's Essential Oneness, which fills all worlds absolutely equally, is concealed and veiled from our comprehension. . . .

Tzimtzum is not meant literally and takes place only in the Or Ein Sof, not in Atzmut: This is the view maintained by Rabbi Shneur Zalman of Liadi and the *Chabad* school as the official chasidic interpretation, since it is a corollary of the Ba'al Shem Tov's commentary on the verse "Forever, O God, Your word stands firm in the heavens" (Psalms 119:89), as will be explained at length below.

Rabbi Shneur Zalman presents several arguments against interpreting the *tzimtzum* literally:

1. Literal withdrawal, as if from place to place, applies only to material objects.[45]
2. To make a distinction between the king himself and his *hashgacha* (the metaphor used by R. Emmanuel Chai Riki) can only be posited of a human king, not of God. God's knowledge of things is not something additional to His Essence. On the contrary, "by knowing Himself, He knows all things."[46] Moreover, His knowledge is not merely "overseeing" from a distance, but actually envelops the object He knows and creates and animates it.[47]
3. A verse states explicitly, "Do I not fill the heavens and earth, says God?" (Jeremiah 23:24).[48] "I" in this context is to be understood literally—"My Essence"—for we have no reason to interpret it otherwise, as will be explained shortly.

---

45. *Tanya, Sha'ar HaYichud veHaEmunah,* chap. 7.
46. Maimonides, *Code, Yesodei HaTorah* 2:9–10.
47. *Tanya,* ad loc.
48. *Tanya, Iggeret HaKodesh,* chap. 25.

4. God's Omnipresence is a matter of uncomplicated faith and solid tradition among Jews of all generations, and they have not tried to find out by rational inquiry exactly how God, who transcends all comprehension, fills the worlds.[49]

Rabbi Shneur Zalman's interpretation of the *tzimtzum*, then, is that the *tzimtzum* takes place in the *Or Ein Sof* only, not in *Atzmut*; and that *tzimtzum* is not to be taken literally as withdrawal, but merely as concealment. Consequently, the *Or Ein Sof* is to be found in the *makom panui* exactly as it was prior to the *tzimtzum*, although what was previously revealed is now concealed by means of the *tzimtzum*. Furthermore, even in the area affected by the *tzimtzum*, the concealment of the *Or Ein Sof* applies only regarding the world, not regarding God Himself, as will be explained below.[50]

One of the arguments presented by those who maintain that the *tzimtzum* is meant literally is that it is in God's power to actually remove Himself from the *makom panui*. To this, two answers may be given:[51]

1. It is certainly possible that God could have removed His *Atzmut* from the *makom panui*, but, in fact, He didn't! This is proved by the verse cited above, "Do I not fill the heavens and earth, says God?" The counter-argument that the verse should not be interpreted literally may be answered as follows: There is a general exegetical rule that states that "no verse is ever excluded from its literal interpretation" (*Shabbat* 63a; *Yevamot* 24a). Because of this rule, the *tzimtzum* should not be taken literally—for if the *tzimtzum* is interpreted literally, the verse must be interpreted allegorically, contradicting the above rule. Alternatively, if the verse

---

49. Ibid.
50. *Sefer HaMa'amarim Melukat*, vol. 4, p. 340.
51. *Mishnat Chabad Tzimtzum*, chap. 4, para. 6.

is interpreted literally, preserving the above exegetical rule, the *tzimtzum* must be interpreted figuratively! Now, which is preferable—to interpret the *tzimtzum* literally and the verse allegorically, or vice versa?[52]

Rabbi Shneur Zalman explains that his interpretation is also supported by the statement of the *Zohar*, "No place is devoid of Him." He explains that this means that, "His Essence and Being, called *Ein Sof* [i.e., *Atzmut*, and not *Or Ein Sof*] . . . completely fills the whole earth within time and space!"[53] Although R. Elijah of Vilna, the leader of the opposition mitnagdic camp, interprets this statement as meaning that no place is devoid of His *hashgacha*, the *Zohar* uses the masculine grammatical form in this expression: *panui Minei* ("no place is devoid of Him"—clearly referring to God) rather than the feminine form *panui Mina* ("no place is devoid of her"), which is the proper form if the intention is to refer to God's *hashgacha*.[54]

2. In addition, the *tzimtzum* cannot be taken as an isolated doctrine. It must be understood in the context of an entire ontological and cosmological system. We explained earlier that chasidic teachings maintain that only "the blessed Emanator, whose Being is of His Essence, and He is not . . . caused by some other cause preceding Himself . . . only He has it in His power and ability to create something out of absolutely naught and nothingness. . . ."[55] Furthermore, the Ba'al Shem Tov interpreted the verse "Forever, O God, Your word stands firm in the heavens" (Psalms 119:89)—as follows: "Your

---

52. *Mishnat Chabad Tzimtzum*, chap. 4, n. 123.

53. *Tanya, Sha'ar HaYichud veHaEmunah*, chap. 7, p. 82b.

54. It is interesting to note that in his commentary to the *Tikkunei Zohar*, R. Elijah does not indicate that he had a different version in which the feminine form was used.

55. *Tanya, Iggeret HaKodesh*, chap. 20, pp. 130a–b.

word," which You uttered, "There shall be a firmament in the midst of the waters . . ." (Genesis 1:6), these very words and letters[56] stand firmly forever within the firmament of heaven and are forever clothed within all the heavens to give them life, as it is written, "The word of our God shall stand firm forever" (Isaiah 40:8), and "His words live and stand firm forever . . ."[57] For if the letters were to depart [even] for an instant, God forbid, and return to their source, all the heavens would become naught and absolute nothingness, and it would be as though they had never existed at all, exactly as before the utterance "There shall be a firmament . . ." And so it is with all created things, in all the upper and lower worlds, and even the physical earth . . . if the letters of the Ten Utterances[58] by which the earth was created during the Six Days of Creation were to depart from it for [even] an instant, God forbid, it would revert to naught and absolute nothingness, exactly as before the Six Days of Creation.[59]

. . . With the withdrawal of the power of the Creator from the thing created, God forbid, it would revert to naught and complete nonexistence. Rather, the Activating Force of the Creator must continuously be in the created thing to give it life and existence.[60]

It follows that had God removed His Essence from this world (*tzimtzum,* interpreted literally), the entire creation would not now exist, for it would have reverted to "naught and complete nonexistence." It is therefore obvious that those who understand

---

56. I.e., the Divine creative force that brings everything into being *ex nihilo.*

57. Morning Liturgy.

58. *Avot* 5:1.

59. Tanya, *Sha'ar HaYichud veHaEmunah,* chap. 1.

60. Ibid., chap. 2.

the *tzimtzum* literally must also disagree with the principle of continuous creation as proposed by the Ba'al Shem Tov.[61]

THE CHABAD VIEW OF *TZIMTZUM*

We are now in a position to explain the view of Rabbi Shneur Zalman of Liadi and his successors regarding the *tzimtzum*.

As mentioned above, Rabbi Shneur Zalman maintains that the entire *tzimtzum* took place in the *Or Ein Sof* and not in *Atzmut*. The effect of the *tzimtzum* is to conceal the *Or Ein Sof* that pervades all of existence, bringing about a *makom panui* that is devoid of the revelation of *Or Ein Sof*, but not of *Atzmut*, and that introduces a limited revelation by way of what is called the *kav*. The "withdrawal" of the *Or Ein Sof* from the *makom panui* is therefore not to be interpreted literally, but merely as conceal-ment.[62] The necessity for this concealment was, in a general sense, that a finite, material world could not exist within the infinite revelation of the *Or Ein Sof*. However, more specifically, several explanations of the necessity for the *tzimtzum* are to be found in *Chabad* texts. Some of them are as follows:[63]

Because of the Loftiness of the *Or Ein Sof* We explained above that there are three levels within the *Or Ein Sof*. Even after the *tzimtzum*, the two higher levels of *Or Ein Sof* transcend the

---

61. The Lubavitcher Rebbe concludes that this inference is somewhat difficult to accept, since the Ba'al Shem Tov's view is based on a primary source—*Midrash Tehillim*, on the verse. He therefore surmises that the contrary opinion must be based on the view that the creation is brought into existence and maintained in existence by God's *hashgacha* and not by His Essence, although this, too, is problematic.

62. *Likkutei Torah, Netzavim*, pp. 49a–b.

63. See *Mishnat Chabad, Tzimtzum*, chap. 3.

worlds completely, for the *tzimtzum* has no effect on them, as will be explained below. Thus, we are dealing here with only the level of light that is relevant to the worlds. Prior to the *tzimtzum*, even the level of *Or Ein Sof* that is relevant to the worlds is infinite, does not have the qualities of higher and lower, beginning and end, and so forth. Accordingly, it, too, is beyond any of the worlds, for even the highest of the worlds is nevertheless limited. Consequently, in order for the worlds to exist as they are at present, the *tzimtzum* was necessary.

Because of the Status of the *Or Hashayach L'Olamot* Prior to the *tzimtzum*, the light that is relevant to the worlds did not exist as a separate level. Rather, it was completely merged within its source.[64] For this reason as well, the *tzimtzum* was necessary, for it brought about the "separation" of the higher levels of *Or Ein Sof* from the lower level, so that this level would be relevant to the worlds.

So That the Worlds Would Exist Prior to the *tzimtzum*, the *Or Ein Sof* filled all of existence. Even though there was already potential for existence, this was actualized only through the *tzimtzum*.

So That the *Sefirot* Could Emerge as Separate Entities Prior to the *tzimtzum*, the *Or Ein Sof* that filled all of existence was absolutely *pashut*—that is, "noncompound and unformed,"[65] and everything was absolutely uniform with no individuating characteristics.[66] Now, even though the potential for individual *sefirot*

---

64. See *Torah Or*, p. 14a, 87b; *Likkutei Torah Pikkudei*, p. 7b; *Sefer HaArachim Chabad*, vol. 3, p. 96ff.

65. *Eitz Chaim Drush Iggulim VeYosher, anaf* 2; *Otzrot Chaim*, beginning.

66. *Sefer HaMa'amarim 5656*, p. 370.

had already been measured out prior to the *tzimtzum*, in a type of measuring out in thought called *hash'ara bekoach*[67] ("measuring in potential everything that was to be in actuality," as mentioned above) nevertheless, the way this existed in thought was completely different from the way God wanted this to be in actuality. Accordingly, the *tzimtzum* was necessary.[68]

As yet, we have not described what actually happened to the *Or Ein Sof* when the *tzimtzum* took place. Rabbi Shneur Zalman explains as follows: The Holy One, blessed is He, *tzimtzum* ("withdrew" or "rescinded," in a figurative sense) the *Or Ein Sof*, so that it would merge back into its source, and remain in a state of potentiality—in Rabbi Shneur Zalman's words: *nichlal ha'Or beMa'or*. (It should be noted that in this context, the term *Ma'or* does not signify *Atzmut*,[69] for *Atzmut* cannot be regarded as the source of the *Or Ein Sof* in the same way that the sun, as a luminary, is the source of its rays, as explained in Chapter 4. Rather, the term *Ma'or* here signifies that level from which the *Or Ein Sof* emerges). The *tzimtzum* is therefore the (figurative) elevation of the *Or Ein Sof* to its former level, prior to its state of revelation. That is, it was returned to the potential to illuminate.

When the *Or Ein Sof* was figuratively "withdrawn" back into its source, so that the light was no longer revealed, *Atzmut*[70] then became "revealed." When Rabbi Shneur Zalman says that *Atzmut* is "revealed," he means that it is revealed as the immutable, omnipres-

---

67. See *Mishnat Chabad Hash'ara beKoach*.

68. *Sefer HaMa'amarim Melukat*, vol. 3, p. 165; *Sha'ar HaYichud*, R. Dovber of Lubavitch, chaps. 10, 11. See also *Sefer HaMa'amarim 5672*, pp. 130–131.

69. See *Sefer HaMa'amarim 5648*, p. 162; *Haga'ot l'Patach Eliyahu 5658*, p. 52.

70. *Torah Or* 14b; *Likkutei Torah*, s.v., chap. 3. Note that the use of the word *Ma'or* in this context is used as a synonym for *Atzmut*.

ent, ineffable *Atzmut*, of whom everyone is aware, and whom no one comprehends,[71] as explained previously in Chapter 4.

It is therefore precisely by way of the *tzimtzum* that *Atzmut* is revealed. That is to say, the awareness of *Atzmut* becomes actualized by way of the *tzimtzum*, for when the *Or Ein Sof* illuminates all of existence, there is more awareness of *Or Ein Sof*, because of its state of revelation, and less awareness of *Atzmut*.[72] Although at present this "revelation" of *Atzmut* is incomprehensible and remains merely as a feeling of awareness, nevertheless, in the messianic era and especially in the time of the Resurrection of the Dead, *Atzmut* will be revealed to everyone, without any obstruction or concealment. At that time "Your teacher shall no longer hide Himself" (Isaiah 30:20)—by way of the *tzimtzum*. That is, this world will become the place "where God can be Himself, at home," as was explained in chapter 5. Furthermore, this is not only regarding God Himself, but also regarding man, "Your eyes shall see your Teacher"—so that "the glory of the Lord shall be revealed and all flesh [even physical flesh] shall see together" (Isaiah 40:5).

However, as explained above, the ultimate purpose of the *tzimtzum* is not to bring about a lack of revelation of the *Or Ein Sof*, even though this reveals the *Atzmut*. On the contrary, the ultimate purpose of the *tzimtzum* is to enable a revelation of *Or Ein Sof* that allows the worlds to exist and allows people to internalize the greatest measure of illumination of which they are capable (while the *Atzmut* is simultaneously revealed as *Atzmut*). We may ask, therefore, how this comes about by way of raising the *Or Ein Sof* into a state of non-illumination? How does the situation of *nichlal ha'Or beMa'or* bring about the existence of finite worlds and vessels?

In order to explain this, we must examine the effect of the *tzimtzum* on each of the three levels of *Or Ein Sof*:

---

71. See *Torah Or* 14b; *Hagahot lePatach Eliyahu 5658*, p. 52.

72. *Sefer HaMa'amarim 5672*, p. 717; *Sefer HaMa'amarim Melukat*, vol. 2, p. 232.

Etzem ha'Or—the essence of the light that merges completely with its Source and is thus unidentifiable—was never in a state of revelation to begin with. Accordingly, one cannot speak of it as being concealed by the *tzimtzum* either. This level of light was therefore untouched by the *tzimtzum*.[73]

Ha'Or she'b'gilui l'Atzmo—the light that is revealed only to Himself, and the purpose of which is to reveal Godliness and bring about a state of total existential nullification. When this level of light was revealed, finite being and worlds could not exist.[74] Furthermore, while this level of light was revealed, the *or hashayach l'olamot* ("light appropriate for creation") was totally flooded by it and it was consequently of no benefit to the worlds. The *tzimtzum* therefore merely concealed this level of light, by raising it into its source so that it would no longer flood the *makom panui* with the revelation of Godliness. The *tzimtzum* is thus described as merely "touching" (*naga bo*) the *Or she'b'gilui l'Atzmo*.

Ha'Or hashayach l'olamot—This is the level of *Or Ein Sof* that is relevant to the worlds, and suffuses each of the worlds, and is revealed within each of them as the Creative Force that brings them into existence and sustains them, each according to its level. Nevertheless, in itself, even this level of light is far too sublime to give rise to material existence, and must be reduced and transformed by way of the *tzimtzum*. In this case, the *tzimtzum* was not mere concealment of the light but such a drastic reduction of the light that all that remained was a mere residue or impression (*reshimu*) of the original light within the *makom panui*.

---

73. *Sefer HaMa'amarim 5666*, p. 195; *Sefer HaMa'amarim 5685*, p. 102.

74. *Sefer HaMa'amarim 5672*, p. 934ff. For further references, see *Mishnat Chabad*, chap. 5.

The explanation of this is as follows: Prior to the *tzimtzum*, the *Or Ein Sof* did not fill all of existence in a way of *hitpashtut* ("extension"). In this sense, it is unlike the flow of a stream of water. A stream of water, in order to irrigate some distant spot, must extend that far. It cannot irrigate that spot by remaining where it is. The obvious corollary of this is that the stream of water is not to be found at all in any place that it does not reach or that it is prevented from reaching. The *Or Ein Sof*, however, filled (and fills) all of existence in a way of *gilui* ("revelation") rather than *hitpashtut* ("extension"). This means that the *Or Ein Sof* is not found in a different place from *Atzmut* but is in the very place in which the *Atzmut* is found[75]—that is, everywhere, for "there is no place devoid of Him." Accordingly, the *Or Ein Sof* did not go anywhere when it ceased to be revealed in the *makom panui* after the *tzimtzum*. It was merely concealed (although so drastically that only a residue of it remains revealed within the *makom panui*).

(*Chabad* sources point out that the very fact that a residue of the light remained within the *makom panui*—the *reshimu*—also indicates that the *tzimtzum* is not a literal withdrawal of the light.)[76]

The *tzimtzum* is therefore not to be regarded as a cessation of *hitpashtut* of the *Or Ein Sof* but merely as a suspension of its *gilui*. This means that the *Or Ein Sof* remains within the *makom panui* even after the *tzimtzum*, and the only difference between before and after *tzimtzum* is in terms of its revelation.[77]

The term *makom panui* is therefore meant metaphorically, not literally. For this reason, it is also referred to as a *makom kadosh*—"a holy place,"[78] for it is precisely within the *makom*

---

75. See *Siddur im Dach*, p. 48aff.

76. See *Likkutei Torah, Behar* 43b; *Derech Mitzevotecha*, p. 134b.

77. Ibid., para. 5.

78. *Sefer HaMa'amarim 5684*, p. 82–83. See also *Likkutei Sichot*, vol. 29, p. 31, n. 39.

panui that God's true unity is to be realized—even within a place that is apparently devoid of God, He is also to be found. This is also the meaning of the midrashic statement[79] explaining the oneness of God:

> Moses placed [located] Him even within *chalalo shel olam* [the *chalal* or *makom panui*], as it says, "The Lord is God in the heavens above, and on the earth below, there is nothing else" (Deuteronomy 39:4). What does "there is nothing else" mean? Even within *chalalo shel olam*![80]

IMMUTABILITY

According to Rabbi Shneur Zalman, the *tzimtzum* took place only in the *Or Ein Sof*—and in the lowest level thereof—and not in *Atzmut*, as explained above. It follows[81] that the *tzimtzum* does not cause any change within *Atzmut*,[82] just as the sun itself is unaffected when its rays are blocked by clouds.[83]

In this regard the verse states, "I, God, have not changed" (Malachi 3:6). This refers to *Atzmut*, in which the *tzimtzum* causes no innovation and which undergoes no change.[84] Nevertheless, one may ask, since the *Or Ein Sof* was concealed or withdrawn to a higher, inscrutable level, does this not imply a change of status? The answer again is that the *tzimtzum* is not a lack of *hitpashtut*, but only a lack of *gilui*, as was explained previously. Accordingly,

---

79. *Devarim Rabbah* 2:28.

80. *Mayim Rabim 5636*, chap. 12; *Sefer HaMa'amarim 5672*, pp. 1333–1334; *Likkutei Sichot*, vol. 29, pp. 26ff.

81. For the following, see, at length, *Mishnat Chabad, Tzimtzum*, chap. 7.

82. *Torah Or*, p. 14b; *Siddur im Dach*, p. 49d.

83. See *Derech Mitzevotecha*, pp. 51a–b.

84. *Siddur im Dach*, p. 49d.

it is self-evident that *Atzmut* is unaffected thereby, just as a person's intellectual ability is unaffected by the fact that he is not thinking at present, or his power of sight is unaffected by the fact that he presently has his eyes closed.

Furthermore, the *tzimtzum* brought about no change in the *Or Ein Sof* either, since it was not removed as such (in the sense of being transferred from one place to another) but was simply concealed. The *Or Ein Sof* therefore remains just as it was, except for the fact that after the *tzimtzum*, it is no longer revealed. This is comparable to a person who stops revealing his thoughts in speech, even though he continues to think. The only change concerns the recipients.[85]

All of the above applies to the *Or Ein Sof* in general. More specifically, not all the three levels of *Or Ein Sof* were affected equally by the *tzimtzum*: The highest level of the *Or Ein Sof*, *Etzem Ha'or*, remains absolutely unaffected. Since this level of *Or Ein Sof* is not in the category of revelation at all, being too sublime to be revealed, it is not appropriate to speak of it as being concealed by the *tzimtzum* either.[86] The second level of the *Or Ein Sof*, *Ha'or she'b'gilui l'Atzmo*, in essence remains unaffected by the *tzimtzum*. Only the aspect of it that was revealed prior to the *tzimtzum* became concealed by the *tzimtzum*. The reason for this is that since this level of light transcends the worlds, the *tzimtzum* does not have the power to constrict the essence of this level of light. All that the *tzimtzum* can do is prevent this level of *Or Ein Sof* from becoming revealed within the *makom panui*. Nevertheless, as far as God's knowledge is concerned, this level of light remains revealed, just as it was prior to the *tzimtzum*.[87]

---

85. *Likkutei Torah, s.v.,* end chap. 3.

86. *Sefer HaMa'amarim 5666,* p. 515; *Sefer HaMa'amarim 5672,* p. 491, 927–928.

87. *Sefer HaMa'amarim 5672,* pp. 934ff; *Vayedaber Elokim 5696,* chap. 4; *Sefer HaMa'amarim 5704,* p. 266.

Even the *Or hashayach l'olamot* ("the light that is relevant to the worlds"), which fills the *makom panui* prior to the *tzimtzum*, is essentially unaffected by the *tzimtzum*. The only difference between prior- and post- *tzimtzum* is that before the *tzimtzum*, the *Or Ein Sof* illuminated the letters of the *reshimu*, whereas after the *tzimtzum*, the *Or Ein Sof* no longer illuminated the letters of the *reshimu*,[88] as mentioned previously. This is comparable, for example, to a person who knows a certain tractate of the Talmud thoroughly. When he is occupied with studying it and explaining it out loud to himself or to someone else, the depth of meaning of the letters of the text before him becomes revealed. However, when he ceases to study the tractate, although he still knows its entire breadth and depth, this remains in a non-revealed state— that is, non-revealed within his speech, or to another person, although he himself still clearly retains all the depth of meaning of the words and letters. Thus, despite the fact that every world that is brought about by the *tzimtzum* contains a different level of Divine revelation, this is only regarding the worlds and not regarding their Creator.

Thus, the state of concealment brought about by the *tzimtzum* only concerns us and doesn't concern God. Just as the *Or Ein Sof* filled all of existence prior to the *tzimtzum*, so, too, does it after the *tzimtzum*, except that now it is concealed so that a finite world can come into existence.

This does not mean to say, however, that the *tzimtzum* is simply a sleight of hand or an imaginary event, for the Torah states clearly that "In the beginning God created . . ."[89] (Genesis 1:1). The creation that came about by way of the *tzimtzum* really exists. Furthermore, even if one wished to interpret this verse allegorically, the body of authoritative Jewish law (*halachah*) takes it as

---

88. *Derech Mitzevotecha*, pp. 136a–b.

89. *Derech Mitzevotecha*, p. 54b; *Sefer HaMa'amarim 5629*, p. 148; *Likkutei Sichot*, vol. 21, pp. 433–434; *Likkutei Sichot*, vol. 19, p. 415.

axiomatic that the world does indeed exist. The *Mishnah*, in Tractate *Sanhedrin* (67a), states: "Two people were picking vegetables [by means of sorcery]. One of them is liable [for the death sentence], and the other is exempt. The one who actually did the deed is liable [for having violated the prohibition of tinkering with spirits], whereas the one who simply used sleight of hand is exempt." This proves that as far as the *halachah* is concerned, the world clearly exists, for if it was merely a "sleight of hand" no one would be liable for reward or punishment.[90] This obviously has bearing on the question of whether chasidic (and more specifically, *Chabad*) philosophy should be categorized as acosmic or not.

Chasidism in general (and *Chabad* Chasidism in particular) has often been branded as pantheistic or acosmic.[91]

Acosmism, loosely defined, maintains that God is the only reality and all else is simply an illusion. An acosmic conception of the world therefore acknowledges only the existence of God and views all other reality as an illusion totally devoid of substance.[92] This challenges empirical experience and conventional criteria. Its basic assumption maintains that there is only a single essence, the Divine Essence, that fills all of existence. All other reality, which appears to be substantial, is merely an illusion, intellectual nearsightedness, and a lie.[93]

In this context, Rabbi Shneur Zalman's *Sha'ar HaYichud v'ha-Emunah* might seem to imply an acosmic position:[94]

> . . . Their existence is nullified in relation to their source, just as the light of the sun is nullified and is considered naught and complete nothingness and is not [even] referred to as "existing" at

---

90. See *HaMelech Bemesibo*, vol. 2, p. 220; *Sefer HaMa'amarim 5629*, p. 143ff; *Mayim Rabim 5636*, chap. 158, et al.

91. See, for example, Professor Gershom Scholem, *Major Trends in Jewish Mysticism*, p. 341.

92. See Rachel Elior, *The Paradoxical Ascent*, p. 49ff.

93. Ibid., p. 54.

94. *Tanya, Sha'ar HaYichud v'ha'Emunah*, p. 78b.

all when it is in its source; only beneath the heavens, where its source is not present [can it be called "existing"]. In the same manner, the term YESH ("existence") can be applied to all created things only as they appear to the corporeal eyes, for we do not see nor comprehend at all the source, which is the spirit of God, that brings them into existence. Therefore, it appears to our eyes that the materiality, grossness, and tangibility of the created things actually exist, just as the light of the sun appears to have actual existence when it is not within its source.

From the above, one can easily conclude that since Godliness, unlike the sun, is everywhere equally, therefore the world is merely an illusion![95] In other words, the world does not exist as the result of a cosmological act but as the result of a psychological act, in which the universe is brought into existence (by way of the *tzimtzum*) only from the point of view of man.[96] However, the truth of the matter is that Chasidism does not move the process of creation into the realm of psychological sleight-of-hand. The intention of the above quote is merely to show that the creation is absolutely contingent, in contrast to the necessary existence of God.[97] As pointed out above, Chasidism adheres to the doctrine of creation *ex nihilo*, with the important corollary that the creative force is always present within the creation and is continuous— "for the fact that they were created during the Six Days of Creation is not sufficient for their continued existence."[98] Accordingly, the creation is an act, and a continuous act at that, not a thing, and it therefore requires the constant input of the Creator in order to exist.[99] Nothing can be more contingent than this.

---

95. Moshe Hallamish, *Mishnato Ha-iyunit*, p. 127.

96. See Elior, *The Paradoxical Ascent*, chap. 11.

97. In fact, to his credit, Hallamish reaches the same conclusion. See *Mishnato ha-iyunit*, pp. 128–129.

98. Ibid., p. 79a. See, at length, *Sha'ar HaYichud v'ha'Emunah*, chap. 2.

99. *Sha'ar HaYichud v'ha'Emunah*, chap. 2.

Furthermore, the persistent reminder throughout *Chabad* litera-ture[100] that the purpose of creation is that "God desired a dwelling place in the lower worlds" clearly refutes any acosmic position.

As for the accusation of pantheism, the entire concept of creation *ex nihilo*, which is a cornerstone of chasidic philosophy, clearly rules out any pantheistic approach. The material world is not a manifestation of His being, for God cannot be consubstan-tial with a universe that was created from nothingness.

Nevertheless, the apparent tendency toward viewing the uni-verse as an illusion must be explained. This subject will be treated in Chapter 9.

THE FINITE WORLDS

We explained earlier that one of the purposes of the *tzimtzum* is to create "vessels" for the *Or Ein Sof*. In this regard, R. Yitzchak Luria states: The *tzimtzum* and reduction of the light enables the formation and revelation of *keilim* ["vessels"],[101] and reveals the root of *din* ["restriction, limitation"].[102]

The purpose of the *tzimtzum*, from this point of view, is to create a void in which the intensity of the *Or Ein Sof* that filled the void prior to the *tzimtzum* has been dimmed, so that finite worlds can come into being where they could not exist previously.

However, the withdrawal (i.e., concealment) of the *Or Ein Sof* is, in and of itself, insufficient to actually bring about a finite creation. It is merely the prerequisite thereof. In order for finite being to exist, a second step was needed. This second phase of the creative process is described as the introduction of a thin beam or line of light, called

---

100. Based, in general, on *Tanya*, chap. 36.
101. *Eitz Chaim, sha'ar 71, anaf 3.*
102. Ibid., *anaf 52.*

the *kav*, into the *chalal*. This *kav* illuminates the *chalal* and is the source of all subsequent emanations. The *kav* is thus a creative and vivifying force, bringing the worlds into being and maintaining their existence. It signifies the immanent revelation of God, as opposed to the infinite, transcendent revelation of God, that is, the *Or Ein Sof*, which envelops and transcends the void.

The *kav* itself subsequently undergoes a number of contractions and concealments, bringing about various planes of reality, referred to as the "worlds" in kabbalistic and chasidic literature. The word for "world" in Hebrew, *olam*, is derived from the word *he'elem*, meaning "concealment." Only when infinite Godliness has been concealed can finite existence come into being. Because Godliness is concealed in various degrees, the existence of manifold planes of reality is brought about. These are known in kabbalistic literature as the five worlds. The higher the world, the greater is its level of revelation of Godliness. The lower the world, the greater the concealment of Godliness. Of course, "there is no place devoid of Him."[103] The essence of God is found everywhere equally, in the highest worlds as in the lowest. The only difference between them is in terms of the revelation of *Or Ein Sof* in them. The higher worlds receive the radiation of the *Or Ein Sof* in a more revealed way than the lower worlds. Although a detailed description of the various worlds, and the *sefirot* that are their structural form, is beyond the scope of the present work, some aspects of these concepts will be examined in the following chapter.

---

103. *Tikkunei Zohar*, p. 122b.

8

TOHU AND TIKKUN—TURMOIL AND RESTITUTION

The origin of the multifarious universe, as well as the origin of evil, is explained at length in Lurianic *Kabbalah*[1] by the doctrine of the breaking of the vessels (*shevirat hakeilim*) of the world of *Tohu*, and is based on several extremely abstruse teachings in the *Zohar*[2] and midrashic sources.[3]

As explained earlier, the *tzimtzum* brings about a radical break between the Creator and the created. Subsequently, a thin ray of light is introduced into the void left by the *tzimtzum*. This thin ray of light, the *kav*, also undergoes various contractions and con-

---

1. Discussed in numerous places, especially *Eitz Chayim, Heichal HaNekudim; Mevoh She'arim, part 2, 2:1–11; Sha'ar HaHakdamot, Derush Be'Olam HaNekudim*, pp. 81–109.
2. Vol. 2, p. 176b; vol. 3, pp. 128a, 135a–b, 142a–b.
3. *Bereishit Rabbah* 3:7, 9:2, 12:15; *Peskita Rabbati* 40.

cealments, bringing about various planes of reality, referred to as the "worlds." These constitute intermediary stages between the infinite light of the *Or Ein Sof* and the finite universe, and make the creation of a finite and complex universe possible.

The actual structure of each of these worlds is constituted by the manifestation of the Divine Attributes known as the *sefirot*— emanations that represent various aspects of Godliness revealed in and to the creation. These are essentially a manifestation of the power of limitation that existed within the *Or Ein Sof* prior to creation and become revealed as a result of the withdrawal of the *Or Ein Sof* by means of the *tzimtzum*. As explained earlier, because the *Or Ein Sof* "had no beginning and no end, but was uniform in every way, when it rose in His will to create worlds," God "measured out within Himself in potential what would exist in the future in actuality."[4] Or, in other words, He "measured out" within Himself how He would bring about a finite existence— prior to actually doing so. This "measuring out" is called in the *Zohar*[5] *galif galifu b'tehiru ila'ah*—"He engraved letters (or, 'engravings') in the Supernal Purity" (the *Or Ein Sof*).[6] These "letters" signify the structuring and formation of the Divine Will prior to the *tzimtzum*, although (prior to the *tzimtzum*) they cannot yet be regarded as the manifestation of His will. They are therefore called only "the potential for limitation." *Chabad* texts refer to these "letters" as the "letters of the *reshimu* ('traces' or 'imprints') prior to the *tzimtzum*."[7]

Prior to the *tzimtzum*, these "letters" are flooded with *Or Ein Sof*, so that the attribute of limitation that they constitute is not

4. *Sefer HaMa'amarim 5666*, pp. 515–517; *Sefer HaMa'amarim 5672*.

5. Vol. 1, p. 15a.

6. See *Hallelu' 5656*, p. 371; *Sefer HaMa'amarim 5677*, p. 18; *Sefer HaMa'amarim 5666*, p. 5–6; *Sefer HaArachim Chabad*, vol. 3, p. 270.

7. *Likkutei Torah Behar*, p. 43c; ibid., *Vayikra, Hosafot*, p. 53b–c; *Or HaTorah Devarim*, pp. 924–925.

actualized but remains a mere potential for limitation. It is only after the *tzimtzum* that these "letters" become actualized as the *sefirot*. One of the functions of the *tzimtzum* is therefore to remove the *Or Ein Sof* that floods these letters so that limitation and finitude can be actualized. From this point of view, the effect of the *tzimtzum* is to prevent the *Or Ein Sof* from illuminating these letters, so that after the *tzimtzum* the letters of the *reshimu* remain as the actualization of the "measuring out" of the Divine Will.

The existence of the *sefirot* in no way implies the dualism of plurality within Divinity, for they are not separate entities from the *Or Ein Sof*. Rather, there is an intrinsic unity between them, as is emphasized in the words of one of the most ancient of kabbalistic texts, the *Sefer Yetzirah*: "The ten *sefirot* are without substance [*bli-mah*]. Their end is wedged in their beginning, and their beginning is wedged in their end—like a flame bound up in the coal. For God is One, and there is no second to Him, and prior to what can you count?"[8]

The same metaphor is restated in the *Zohar*: "The Holy One, blessed is He, emits ten crowns, supernal holy crowns, with which He crowns Himself, and in which He vests Himself. He is they, and they are He, just as the flame is bound up in the coal, and there is no division there."[9] All differentiation is from our perspective and relative to our knowledge only, while above all is One; all is set in one balance, unvarying and eternal, as it is written, "I, God, have not changed" (Malachi 3:6).[10]

There are two basic schemes in the emanation of the *sefirot* after the *tzimtzum*:[11] As was mentioned before, a thin ray of light (the

---

8. *Sefer Yetzirah* 1:7.

9. Vol. 3, p. 70a.

10. See *Zohar*, vol. 2, p. 176a; *Tikkunie Zohar*, Introduction, p. 17a; *Pardess Rimonim* 5:4.

11. See *Etz Chaim*, 1:2–5, 2:1; *Sha'ar HaHakdamot*, sections 4, 5; *Likkutei Torah, Bamidbar* 37c.

kav) is introduced into the void left by the *tzimtzum*. The *kav* does not traverse the void (*chalal*) immediately, from the circumference to its center. Rather, as it enters the *chalal*, it revolves parallel to the *chalal's* perimeter, around its inside, thus establishing a concentric sphere within it. This first concentric sphere is called *keter*, the "crown." Subsequently, the *kav* once again revolves around the inside perimeter of the sphere of *keter*, thus forming a second concentric circle, between *keter* and the *chalal*. This sphere is called *chochmah*. The *kav* continues revolving, forming one sphere within the other, gradually descending to the tenth and final sphere, at the center of the *chalal*—*malchut*. This is called the scheme of *iggulim*, or "concentric circles," wherein each sphere is essentially distinct from the ones above and below it.

A subsequent scheme of *sefirot*, called *yosher*, was then emanated. They have the appearance of a man standing upright[12] and are analogous to a man who has several distinct, but symbiotic organs, working in harmony with each other and forming a single body.[13] Furthermore, these *sefirot* combine together to form "visages"—*partzufim*.[14] The most important feature of this scheme of *sefirot* is that they form a harmonious whole, rather than remaining independent entities as in the scheme of *iggulim*. The significance of this difference will be discussed later.

TOHU AND TIKKUN

The original scheme of the *sefirot*, *iggulim*, and the subsequent scheme, *yosher*, are synonymous with the terms *tohu* and *tikkun*

---

12. See *Pardess Rimonim* 6:3; *Etz Chaim* 1:1. The term *yosher* is derived from the verse "God made man upright [*yashar*]" (*Kohelet* 7:29).

13. See *Zohar*, vol. 1, p. 134b; *Etz Chaim* 1:2.

14. *Tikkunei Zohar* 17a; *Zohar, Sifra d'Tzniuta*.

respectively. The former term, *tohu*, is taken from a biblical verse (Genesis 1:1ff):

> In the beginning of God's creating the heavens and the earth, the earth was inconceivably void [*tohu*], and there was darkness upon the surface of the depths. The Sovereignty of God hovered [*merachefet*] over the surface of the waters. God said, "There shall be light," and there was light. . . .

The verses thus indicate that Godliness was not revealed in a comprehensible way on that plane (it was "inconceivably void") but only in a chaotic form; and that the Sovereignty of God merely "hovered" over its surface, without settling and vesting itself within that world. It is for this reason that God said of this world, "It does not please Me . . ."[15] Technically, the inability of the world of *tohu* to reveal Godliness in an orderly and settled way is because the *sefirot* of that world were unformed and unordered points. As mentioned above, the *sefirot* of *iggulim* were emitted as separate, individual attributes that had no interrelationship or mutual inclusion. Each of these *sefirot* was thus a highly concentrated seminal point of light, so that each of them manifested itself in its purest form—*chesed* was pure *chesed* without any admixture of *gevurah*; *gevurah* was pure *gevurah* without any admixture of *chesed*, and so on.

This inability of the *sefirot* of *tohu* to form a mutual symbiotic relationship was the cause of their breakage, as is explained in the Lurianic doctrine of *sheviras hakeilim*—the "breaking of the vessels,"[16] also hinted at in the words, "The Sovereignty of God hovered [*merachefet*] over the surface of the waters," and in the mystical account of the eight kings of Edom who each ruled and died. This took place prior to the existence of the world of

---

15. *Bereishit Rabbah* 3:7, 9:2.

16. *Eitz Chaim, Heichal haNekudim* (especially, *sha'ar* 8ff.); *Mevoh She'arim*, vol. 2, 2:1–11.

tikkun—"before there reigned any king over the children of Israel,"[17] that is, the world of *tikkun*. This latter world "pleased God"[18] and is alluded to in the words, "God said, 'There shall be light,' and there was light. . . ."

Each of the *sefirot* of the world of *tohu* were, on their own, unable to contain the highly concentrated and very powerful energy that flooded them; and they shattered, producing 288 shards, or sparks, that fell from their spiritual level (this is akin to death) and became embedded in what would be lower levels of creation. The entire process is alluded to in the word *merachefet*, which is a word compounded of *rapach* (having the numerical value of 288) and *met*—"died." As these shards of the *sefirot of tohu* fell downwards, they broke down further into increasingly smaller particles. Not only did the fragments become more numerous as they continued to fall, but they also became coarser. The more refined shards were assimilated into the world of *Atzilut*; subsequent shards that could not be absorbed in *Atzilut* fell further and were absorbed into the worlds of *Beriah* or *Yetzirah*. The coarser the shards, the lower they fell, until eventually, the coarsest shards fell into the world of *Assiyah*. These fragments are responsible for the multifariousness of the creation and also for the existence of evil. They form what is called, in kabbalistic terms, the "shells" or "husks"—a symbol of the superficiality and insensitivity that characterizes evil.

However, it should not be assumed that there was some accidental flaw in the world of *tohu* and that this is why it disintegrated. On the contrary, this was precisely part of the Divine Plan. Since the shattering of the vessels of the world of *tohu* allows for the possibility of evil, man is provided with an opportunity to exercise free choice. Furthermore, through the labor of refining and elevating these sparks, level by level, to their

---

17. Genesis 36:31; 1 Chronicles 1:43.
18. *Bereishit Rabbah* 3:7, 9:2.

original level of sanctity (called *birur hanitzotzot*), man earns spiritual reward.

Man has been placed in the realm in which darkness and evil prevail, in order to affect the refinement and elevation of the "holy sparks" that became embedded in the physical world as a result of the shattering of the world of *tohu*. His mission is to disencumber the sparks of holiness from their shells of evil by way of Torah and *mitzvahs*, as will be discussed at length in Chapter 11.

9

THE ONENESS OF GOD AND THE SPIRITUALITY OF MATTER

In our previous discussion we examined the reasons for, and the process of, creation. Although we examined these ideas at length, we did not analyze some of their important ramifications: How we can reconcile the multifarious creation with the oneness of God? What is the nature of this creation—does it exist outside of Him and therefore imply a duality? Or does it exist within Him and therefore imply corporeality within God?

THE ONENESS OF GOD

Probably the most fundamental principle of Judaism is the belief in the unity and oneness of God. In his *Sefer HaMitzvot* (*mitzvah* 2), Maimonides formulates this principle as the belief that He who brought existence into being, the First Cause of everything, is One, as the verse states "Hear, Israel, the Lord is our God, the Lord is One . . ." (Deuteronomy 6:4) From his words, we understand that this commandment forbids us to believe in partnership (*shittuf*, in Hebrew)—that is, we are forbidden to believe that God has any "partners" in creation. Although the nations of the world are permitted to believe in other powers as well, Jewish monotheism maintains, as a basic principle, that He is the sole Creator of all of existence.[1]

The *Zohar*,[2] however, interprets the declaration of unity—in the verses "Hear O Israel, the Lord our God, the Lord, is One" and "Know this day and take unto your heart that the Lord is God. In the heavens above and on the earth below, there is nothing else" (Deuteronomy 4:39)— somewhat differently.[3] The two appellations, "Lord" (tetragammaton) and "God" (Elokim), explains the *Zohar*, are essentially one. The former Name indicates infinite revelation and expansion without any limitation whatsoever, whereas the latter Name is indicative of the attribute of severity and restriction, concealing and contracting the infinity of the former in the form of the *tzimtzum*, as discussed earlier. The latter Name (Elokim) is also the source of multiplicity and immanence (God within creation), whereas the former is indicative of unity and transcendence, (God as He transcends creation). Nevertheless, the *Zohar* states categorically that they are absolutely one.

Chabad texts[4] clarify the meaning of the *Zohar*'s statement by way of an analogy. A human being also has the power of revelation and the power of limitation and concealment. The

---

1. See *Likkutei Amarim Tanya*, chaps. 20–23.

2. Vol. 1, p. 25a, in *Raya Mehemna*; Introduction to *Zohar*, vol. 1, p. 12a. See also vol. 2, 25a (*Raya Mehemna*).

3. The following is based on the explanation found in *Derech Mitzevotecha, Achdut Hashem*, p. 59bff.; *Veyadata, Moscow 5657*.

4. *Veyadata, Moscow 5657*, p. 7.

power of thought, for example, is capable of producing an endless stream of thoughts. However, it also has the capacity to limit and define concepts, for every concept must have some limitations and must be categorized in some way if it is to be understood at all. Similarly, a teacher must possess the ability to conceal and limit his own understanding of a concept in order to instruct perhaps by way of an analogy, his students who are not yet at the level of understanding to grasp all the details and ramifications of the idea the way the teacher understands it. In both of these examples, the source of the concept is the very same source that limits it. Although the teacher presents the student with an analogy drawn from common experience to illustrate his point, the teacher's own understanding of the concept is in no way obscured by the analogy he uses. The usefulness of the analogy is that it enables the student to understand the concept by comparing it to matters that are within the realm of his own experience. If the analogy is a good one, the student will begin to understand the teaching to which the analogy alludes.

In exactly the same way, these two Divine Names also derive from the identical Source, God Himself. Just as the power of infinite revelation is drawn from His Essence, so, too, the power of concealment and contraction is also drawn from His Essence.[5] Thus, both Divine Names are in reality two different manifestations of divine energy that stem from the identical source.[6] This is the *Zohar's* explanation of the unity of God—that two apparently opposing forces, which led other religions to posit a dual existence, are in reality two sides of the same coin.

---

5. *Veyadata*, ibid. See also Rabbi Meir Ibn Gabbai's *Avodat HaKodesh* 1:8.

6. See also *Tanya, Shaar HaYichud v'HaEmunah*, chaps. 6–7.

BEING AND NOTHINGNESS

The Ba'al Shem Tov, the founder of Chasidism, explains the oneness and unity of God in an even deeper sense,[7] on the basis of a concept we explained earlier: Because the world is created *ex nihilo*, the continued existence of the world must be the product of a constant input of divine energy. This divine energy is none other than the ten utterances through which the world was created originally[8] and through which it continues to be created at every moment, and which are its true existence.

Of course, this concept of speech is only an anthropomorphic analogy.[9] Accordingly, the limitations of human speech do not apply to Divine Speech. When a person utters a word, the breath emitted in speaking is something that can be sensed and perceived as a thing apart, separated from its source. But, regarding the Holy One, blessed is He, His speech is united within Himself in absolute union, comparable to the way a person's speech and thought are united within himself while they are still *in potentia* in his wisdom and intellect, where they are totally united with their source—the wisdom and intellect in the brain.

This is true even after His speech has already become materialized in the creation of the worlds, just as it was united within Himself before the worlds were created, for there is nothing outside of Him, and there is no place devoid of Him.[10]

Rabbi Shneur Zalman of Liadi takes this teaching even further. He explains at length that the entire physical creation is not the

---

7. *Tanya*, chap. 20. See also *Tanya, Shaar HaYichud v'HaEmunah*, chap. 1ff.

8. *Pirkei Avot* 5:1.

9. See *Berachot* 40a.

10. *Tikkunei Zohar, tikkun* 57.

independent existence it appears to be. Although this is the way it appears to us, this is only because we do not see the divine energy that brings physical creation into being and maintains its existence. In comparison with this divine energy, our existence is as if absolutely nothing. He explains this[11] by way of an analogy: The rays of the sun shine down upon earth and upon all its inhabitants. The sun's rays are the radiance and light that spread out from the body of the sun and are visible to all as it gives light to the earth and our solar system. Since light diminishes and dissipates the further it travels, logically then, if the sun's rays shine here, some 93 million miles away from their source, they must be much brighter at their source—the sun's surface. However, if we were standing on the surface of the sun, we would, in fact, see no rays, because where the sun itself exists, its rays are completely and absolutely swallowed up in the brightness and radiance of the sun itself and are regarded as naught and complete nothingness. They are absolutely nonexistent in relation to the body of the sun, which is the source of this light and radiance, since this light and radiance are merely the illumination that shines out from the body of the sun itself. It is only in the space of the universe and down here on earth, where the sun itself is not present, that this light and radiance appears to us to have actual existence. Only here can the terms *yesh* ("being" or "existence") be applied to them at all. However, when they are in their source, in the body of the sun, the term *yesh* cannot be applied to them at all, and they can only be called naught and nonexistent. There, the rays of the sun are indeed naught and absolutely nonexistent, for there, within their source (the body of the sun), only the sun itself gives light, and there is nothing besides it.

Only the *tzimtzum* conceals from us the fact that we are constantly within our Source, and that our existence is always totally nullified, and that there is nothing besides God.

---

11. *Tanya, Shaar HaYichud v'HaEmunah*, chap. 3.

Thus, according to Rabbi Shneur Zalman, not only does God have no partners, and not only do all opposing forces have but one source, and not only is existence completely and totally dependent on the divine energy that brings it into being, but the world itself is also one with God, since the existence of the entire creation is absolutely nullified in His existence. In terms of the analogy used by the Baal Shem Tov: The words of God that bring the existence of the universe into being are always within God and never leave Him. Not only does the world have no independent significance or a life of its own, being completely dependent on God's life-giving force—the world has no independent existence at all because it never "leaves" God.

We must therefore conclude that there is only God, as the verse states: "And you shall know this day, and take it to your heart, that the Lord is God in the heavens above and on the earth below, there is nothing else" (Deuteronomy 4:39). Regarding the last two words in the verse, *ain od*—"there is nothing else," or, "there is no other"—Rabbi Shneur Zalman explains[12] that *od* in Hebrew signifies a secondary or subsidiary existence. Thus the words *ain od* tell us that the world does not even have the status of *od*—a secondary existence—in the presence of God. In comparison to the soul, the body is also referred to as *od*,[13] for without the soul there would merely be a lifeless body, and therefore we call it a secondary existence.[14] But the world has nothing of its own to allow us to consider it even a secondary existence. Nevertheless, as pointed out earlier, this should not be regarded as the acosmism mentioned previously. What we have proved is merely that the world is entirely contingent upon God—not that it does not exist or that it is simply a dream. In other words:

---

12. *Tanya, Shaar HaYichud v'HaEmunah*, chap. 1.
13. See Psalms 104:33, 146:2, Commentaries.
14. *Tanya, Shaar HaYichud v'HaEmunah*, chap. 6, p. 80b–81a.

The *tzimtzum* and concealment is only for the lower [worlds], but in relation to the Holy One, blessed be He, "Everything before Him is considered as actually naught,[15] just like the light of the sun is in the sun." Similarly, "just as before the worlds were created, there was no existence besides His, exactly so now, too, so to speak [it is as if the worlds do not exist] because even though the world and everything in it exist, they are not the existence which the eye sees as real, for they can only be called naught and nonexistent."[16]

On the other hand, this is not a classical case of panentheism, either—the world does not exist within God, for at the level that may be termed "within God," the worlds do not exist at all. As Rabbi Shneur Zalman puts it:

Their existence is nullified in relation to their source, just as the light of the sun is nullified and is considered naught and complete nothingness and is not [even] referred to as "existing" at all when it is in its source; only beneath the heavens, where its source is not present [can it be called "existing"]. In the same manner, the term *yesh* ("existence") can be applied to all created things only as they appear to the corporeal eyes, for we do not see nor comprehend the source at all, which is the spirit of God that brings them into existence. Therefore, it appears to our eyes that the materiality, grossness, and tangibility of the created things actually exist, just as the light of the sun appears to have actual existence when it is not within its source. . . ."[17]

It is possibly for this reason that Maimonides translates *ain od* in his *Code*[18] as meaning that there is no other existence as true as God's.

---

15. *Zohar*, vol. 1, p. 11b.
16. *Derech Mitzevotecha*, p. 62a.
17. *Tanya, Shaar HaYichud v'HaEmunah*, chap. 3, p. 78b.
18. *Yesodei HaTorah* 1:4.

10

Divine Providence (Hashgacha Pratit) in the View of Maimonides and the Ba'al Shem Tov

One of the fundamental principles of Judaism is that God watches everything that man does and cares about what he does.[1] This doctrine is also known as individual Divine providence (or, *hashgacha pratit*). The classical formulation of this doctrine is stated by Maimonides in his Thirteen Principles and also in his

---

1. See the tenth of Maimonides' *Thirteen Principles of Faith*.

Code:[2] "God knows all of man's deeds and thoughts. It is thus
written (Psalms 33:15), 'He has molded every heart together, He
understands what each one does.'" Maimonides explains further[3]
that this principle stands in direct contradiction to those who say
that "God has abandoned His world" (Ezekiel 9:9), for "everything that exists (with the exception of God Himself), exists only
because God gives it existence,"[4] as we explained in the previous
chapter. Moreover,

> it is because God knows Himself, that He knows everything, and
> therefore, nothing is hidden from Him. This knowledge is not
> something that can be separated from His Essence. In this way, it is
> very different from our knowledge. For our knowledge is not the
> same as our identity. But in the case of God, He, His knowledge, and
> His existence are One. They are One in every possible way and in the
> fullest definition of unity. . . .[5]

From the above, it is clear that Divine providence is more than
merely "overseeing" the creation from above. It is integrally
bound up with the continued existence of creation. If this is so in
Maimonides' view, how much more is it true of the Ba'al Shem
Tov's view of Divine providence, which is a necessary corollary of
his view[6] regarding the omnipresence of God, even within the
area described in *Kabbalah* as the *makom panui*—"no place is
devoid of Him"[7]—and his view[8] regarding "continuous creation."
Since God is everywhere, and He constantly utters the ten utterances
that bring every detail of creation into being, there is no possibility

---

2. *Yesodei HaTorah* 2:10.
3. In his *Commentary to the Mishnah*.
4. *Code, Yesodei HaTorah* 2:9.
5. *Code, Yesodei HaTorah* 2:10.
6. Rabbi M. M. Schneerson, *Igrot Kodesh*, vol. 18, p. 206.
7. *Tikkunei Zohar, tikkun* 57.
8. Rabbi M. M. Schneerson, *Igrot Kodesh*, vol. 2, p. 394.

of a "random" event, or indeed of any object existing "outside" of God's flow of life-force.

Let us examine the Ba'al Shem Tov's doctrine of individual Divine providence in greater detail. Whereas Maimonides maintains[9] that individual Divine providence applies only to man, whereas the rest of creation is guided by general Divine providence, the Ba'al Shem Tov maintains that individual Divine providence applies to each and every created thing.

For the Ba'al Shem Tov, not only does God watch over everything that man does and over every detail of his life, but every detail of the entire creation, even the way a leaf is blown about by the wind, is all guided by Divine providence.[10] One of the ramifications of the Ba'al Shem Tov's explanation is that God Himself is involved in each and every detail of creation, not only in that which concerns man,[11] since everything partakes of His unity, and nothing stands outside of it, as we explained above.

The Ba'al Shem Tov explains further that not only is each and every detail of creation, and whatever events take place within all of creation, meant to be, but each and every detail is also an integral part of God's total plan for all of creation. This is analogous to a puzzle, in which even the smallest piece is still part of the puzzle and helps to complete the entire puzzle. If there is

---

9. *Guide*, part 3, chap 17.

10. See *Keter Shem Tov*, (Kehot Publication Society), addenda para. 19ff. *Likkutei Sichot*, vol. 8, p. 277ff.

11. In fact, although this doctrine was emphasized by the Ba'al Shem Tov, its roots can be found in the statements of talmudic Sages, as in the view of Rabbi Yochanan in *Chullin*, 63a. See Rashi, ad loc. Some authorities add that contrary to popular belief, this does not contradict Maimonides' view of personal Divine providence. See Rabbi Dovber Schneuri's *Derech Chaim*, 13a–b, (Kehot Publication Society); *Shaarei Emunah* (Kehot Publication Society 5751 [1991]), p. 91ff. See also *Shomer Emunim*, close to the end; *Eilimah Rabbati*, Rabbi Moses Cordovero, *Ein Kol Tamar* 5:1.

one little detail missing, then the whole puzzle is incomplete. The same is true of God's world. Each and every detail of every creature, and every event within creation is a part of a master plan, and it performs its unique function in fulfilling the purpose of the entire creation, just as each limb and organ of the human body has its function and importance in the proper functioning of the whole body. Hence, each event is necessary, and there is a perfect order in which events occur. Of course, the manner in which everything fits together is inaccessible to human understanding.

We find a similar concept in reference to the Torah. Of all the matters written about in the Torah, we might assume that the commandments are the most important; and of the commandments, the Ten Commandments are surely the most consequential. Furthermore, of the Ten Commandments, the first two, which God Himself communicated directly to the Jewish people, are of the greatest significance. In contrast, we might assume that the stories of the Torah are of lesser importance, and particularly the stories concerning wicked people, such as Esau and Bilaam. Yet this is incorrect, for we find that each and every letter of each and every word in the Torah is equally holy. All of the Torah came from God, as Maimonides explains in the eighth and ninth of his Thirteen Principles of Faith. Therefore, all are equally holy. If one letter or word is missing from a Torah scroll, then the entire scroll is regarded as blemished, and one may not recite the required blessing over it. For each and every letter and word is a part of the entire puzzle.

LEVELS OF DIVINE PROVIDENCE

From the Ba'al Shem Tov's explanation of Divine providence—that not only is everything Divine providence, but the existence of everything in the world, and everything that happens in the world, is part of the divine plan—it follows that all things and all events in the world are interconnected. When a leaf shakes in the wind, when, how, and in which direction it shakes is part of the general puzzle. If this event did not take place, it would affect the whole world and everything that existed, exists, and will exist. All of it is affected because everything is connected to the general purpose of creation.

However, even according to the Ba'al Shem Tov's explanation, there is a fundamental difference between the Divine providence that oversees all of creation, including the minutest details of it, and the Divine providence that guides the Jewish people, in even the minutest detail. This is because of their role in fulfilling the ultimate purpose of creation:

Although all creations were brought into existence by God, nevertheless, He chose only the Jewish people from among all the nations.[12] This is also the meaning of the statement of our Sages[13] that the entire universe was created for the sake of Torah and the people of Israel. This implies that all the rest of creation is simply a means to an end—the fulfillment of God's purpose in creating the world, which is for the sake of the Torah and the people of Israel. However, the Torah and the people of Israel are not a means to an end, but the end in itself. They are the purpose of creation! This means that God chose them for themselves, not for the sake of fulfilling some other task or purpose.

This can be explained at greater length. Because each and every creation in the universe (other than the Torah and the Jewish people) has no purpose other than to serve God, each and every individual creation's importance is based upon its purpose—to what extent it participates in, and adds to, the ultimate purpose of creation. This can be understood by way of an analogy to the

---

12. Compare the blessing recited prior to the Torah reading ". . . Who chose us from among all the nations . . ."; see also Malachi 1:2.

13. Rashi, Genesis 1:1.

body. Although each and every limb, sinew, bone, and organ is equally part of the body, and makes up the entire body, there are nevertheless levels of importance among the limbs, organs, and so forth. The brain is the most important organ, and then the heart, and then the other limbs upon which a person's life depends. Although each and every organ and limb serves a purpose, the nails and hair, for example, are far less important than any other part of the body, for the life of the body does not depend on them at all. In the same way, different parts of creation are more or less important in fulfilling the divine plan, depending upon the extent to which they serve the Torah and the Jewish people.

However, just as God Himself does not "serve a purpose" (i.e., He is not here for the sake of something else, but is because He is), in the same way the Jewish people and the Torah are not here for some other purpose but are themselves the purpose, for this is what God chose. Accordingly, every single detail of the Torah, and every single individual and all the events that take place in the life of every individual Jew, are also an end in themselves, not a means to an end. And therefore, every detail is of equal importance to God. Accordingly, Divine providence for the Jewish people is equal for every Jew (no matter how righteous he is) because God chose the Jewish people in their entirety. The Divine providence that guides the Jewish people thus applies to every single detail of each individual Jew's life, and each and every detail of his life is guided by His providence in equal measure (although this might not be evident in a revealed way).

This is not so with the details of the rest of creation, which gain importance only to the extent to which they serve the ultimate purpose. Just as we find that when a person wants something, and he has a definite picture of what he wants, then every little detail in what he wants, he wants equally. He needs the whole thing in total. If one of those things is missing, then he does not have what he wants. The same principle applies to the Torah. If one single letter or word is defective, the entire Torah is defective and may not be read from in public, irrespective of whether the word, or letter of the word is part of "I am the Lord your God," or part of the list of Esau's descendants, or part of a description of nonkosher animals. The same is true regarding the commandments of the Torah. On one hand, we find that there are different levels of commandments. Some commandments are called minor and others major. Yet the Torah says that one should not weigh and count which commandments are more important than others, because they are all equal[14] in that they are all God's will. Thus, if a convert to Judaism wishes to observe 612 of the 613 commandments, he is not accepted as a convert—until he accepts the Torah in its entirety![15] The same principle applies to a person who says that although he believes in God and that God gave us the commandments, he does not believe that a certain detail of the Torah is from God. It is as if he denies the entire Torah. There is no difference whether he denies the Ten Commandments or he denies any other word in the Torah.

PART OF GOD ABOVE

There is an even deeper explanation of the Divine providence that oversees the Jewish people. A verse[16] states that the Jewish people are a part of God Himself, just as a child is derived from the essence of his father. This goes even further than saying that the children of Israel are the chosen people. As soon as one uses the word "chosen," one implies that there are two things. There is the one who chooses, and there is what he chooses. The Maggid of Mezritch writes[17] that the Jewish people were engraved

---

14. *Tanchuma, Eikev* 2. See *Avot*, chap. 2:1.
15. *Bechorot* 30b; Rambam, *Issurei Biya* 14:8.
16. Deuteronomy 32:9.
17. *Or Torah*, part 2, p. 3.

in God's thought even before the world was created, even before the individual soul of a Jewish person was created as a separate entity. Accordingly, the Divine providence that oversees the Jewish people is not something outside of them. Rather, it is an integral part of their being since they are part of God Himself.

In a similar vein, the Ba'al Shem Tov said,[18]"When you grasp a part of *Atzmut* [the Essence of God], you grasp the entire Essence." Because the Essence is found totally in every part of the Essence. When you grasp part of the Essence, you are really holding onto it all.

We find a parallel to this concept in Jewish law. There is a law that states that if a person is involved in fulfilling a commandment, he is exempt from doing any other commandments.[19] Chasidic philosophy explains that the inner reason that he is exempt from doing any other commandments is that when he is observing one commandment he is really observing all them, for they are all, equally, the essential will of God. If he is fulfilling the will of God by observing one commandment—since, "when you grasp a part of the Essence, you grasp the entire Essence"—he therefore fulfills all the others as well.

In a similar sense, we find that the soul of a Jewish person is regarded as a whole world, to the extent that we sometimes find that the soul of one person is just as important as an entire group of people.[20]

The *halachah*[21] presents the following scenario: An enemy captures a group of Jews and demands that they surrender one of them, who will be put to death. The enemy threatens the group that if they refuse to surrender that individual, then the entire group will be put to death. The *halachah* states clearly that the

---

18. *Keter Shem Tov*, addenda para. 116.
19. *Sukkah* 25a
20. *Mishnah Sanhedrin*, 37a.
21. Authoritative and binding Jewish law.

group may not give up the life of that individual to save the lives of the group. Chasidic philosophy explains that the reason for this ruling is that since every Jewish soul is of the Essence of God, giving up one Jewish person is like giving up the entire Jewish people. Because again, "when you grasp a part of the Essence, you grasp the entire Essence."

With this explanation, we can understand a much deeper concept. The Divine providence that guides the Jewish people is not only that God watches over every detail, and not only that all of the details are equally important in the fulfillment of the divine plan, but that when God watches over even a single detail, it is His Essence watching over every detail, and in His guidance of even the minutest detail, all of His Essence is expressed. This type of Divine providence is unique to the Jewish people.

CONCEALED PROVIDENCE

One may ask, however, if the same principle applies to wicked people as well? Does Divine providence guide them and guard them to the same extent that it guides and guards the righteous? Chasidic texts explain[22] that although the source of Divine providence is exactly the same for every Jew, on an individual basis, the workings of Divine providence may be either revealed or hidden, as a result of the individual's actions. This is the meaning of the verse, "I will conceal my face on that day."[23] The verse explains that as a result of sin, God's providence becomes concealed. Although it still guides the errant Jew, he is not aware of it. Nevertheless, this applies only on an individual basis, but not to the people as a whole, who are always guided by revealed Divine providence.

---

22. *Shaarei Emunah*, p. 94.
23. Deuteronomy 31:18.

It must be pointed out, however, that even according to those views that maintain that individual Divine providence applies only to mankind, and not to any other creatures, this is only in terms of God's guidance, but not in terms of God's knowledge, as the author of the Ikkarim[24] writes:

> It is absolutely unquestionable that His knowledge encompasses everything in existence, and every event in all of existence, and nothing whatsoever is hidden from Him. Nevertheless, His providence does not guide the animal world (and all the more so the plant and inanimate worlds) on an individual basis, to reward or punish them for their deeds. Rather, He oversees the species, not the individuals.[25]

REVEALED AND HIDDEN PROVIDENCE

In fact, chasidic authors[26] point out that the concept of Divine providence, as explained by the Ba'al Shem Tov (that there is individual Divine providence for animals, plants, and inanimate matter, as well as for man) does not necessarily contradict the definition of Divine providence as explained by Maimonides (that individual Divine providence does not apply to animals, plants, and inanimate matter, but only to man). This is because there are, in a general sense, two types of Divine providence:[27] (1) Revealed individual Divine providence, which is not concealed by what

---

24. Rabbi Yosef Albo (d. circa 1420). The *Sefer HaIkkarim* is a commentary to Maimonides' Thirteen Principles.

25. *Ikkarim* 4:7.

26. *Derech Chaim, Shaar HaTeshuvah*, chap. 9. See also *Likkutei Sichot*, vol. 9, p. 181.

27. *Likkutei Sichot*, vol. 18, p. 199; *Hitvaaduyot* 5745, vol. 3, p. 1836.

appears to be the logical result of natural events and the laws of nature. Maimonides maintains that this type of providence is dependent on the level to which a person's thoughts and understanding cleave to God, and it does not apply to animals, plants, and inanimate matter, or to the wicked who separate themselves from God. (2) Providence that is hidden and concealed within the workings of nature and natural law. This type of providence applies to all aspects of creation, including animals, plants, and inanimate matter. This is the Ba'al Shem Tov's approach.

Hence, even according to Maimonides, there is a form of Divine providence that guides the wicked as well. However, this Divine providence is clothed in what appears to be natural events, and it therefore remains unrecognized, so that it is not clearly seen how each and every detail and event comes from the Holy One, blessed is He. This does not contradict Maimonides' view that a wicked person leaves himself at the mercy of "random" events, for it is part of God's plan that Divine providence is concealed (although not removed) from the wicked, resulting in the apparent randomness of events. Nevertheless, revealed Divine providence also operates—as regards the species, but not the individual, as Maimonides maintains.[28]

It is possible that the view adhered to by the Ba'al Shem Tov was even acknowledged by Maimonides, although he did not propound it openly because it falls into the category of the secrets of Torah, which must find the right time and climate to be revealed.[29]

---

28. See *Derech Chaim, Shaar HaTeshuvah*, chap. 9.
29. See *Likkutei Sichot*, vol. 30; *Sichat Yud Tet Kislev.*

HOW DOES GOD KNOW?

This brings us to a further statement mentioned earlier—that God knows all of man's deeds and thoughts. What does "knowing" mean, as far as God is concerned? How does He know? Maimonides writes that everything that exists, besides the Creator Himself, exists only by virtue of the truth of His existence. By knowing Himself, God knows everything, and nothing is hidden from Him.[30] He adds that this knowledge is not something separate from Him—rather, the Creator, His existence, and His knowledge are all totally one, unlike man, whose knowledge is not part of his essence but is acquired from outside of himself. We must therefore conclude that He is the Knower, the known, and the knowing, and all are one. This can neither be expressed in words, nor clearly understood.

The Maharal of Prague,[31] among others, disagree with Maimonides' statement that God's knowledge is of His Essence, for this imposes a definition and limitation on His Essence, which is infinite and therefore cannot be defined or limited in any way, even by something noncorporeal, such as "knowledge." The Maharal explains that this is why we call God "the Holy One, blessed is He," not "the intellect, blessed is He,"—because "holy" means "removed and exalted," so that no definition or limitation is applicable. Therefore, the Maharal concludes that intellect or knowledge is only a creation of God, and whenever it says in the Torah that "God knows," it is equivalent to saying "God said," or "God made"—which means that God created the attribute of knowing, not that He Himself is the knowing. The exact details of their argument, however, need not concern us now.

---

30. *Code, Yesodei HaTorah* 2:9–10; see also *Guide for the Perplexed*, part 3, chaps. 20, 21.

31. See, for example, the Maharal of Prague, Rabbi Yehudah Loewe, in his *Book of Divine Power*, Second Introduction.

In his *Tanya*,[32] Rabbi Shneur Zalman of Liadi explains that Jewish mysticism (*Kabbalah*) agrees with Maimonides' view, that God is the Knower, the known, and the knowing, all at once. Nevertheless, the Maharal's contention—that He cannot be characterized in this way—is also correct. Neither view is wrong in its proper context, for each view, in fact, refers to a different concept.

The explanation of this is as follows: There is God as He is in Himself, transcending any revelation or manifestation—this is what we defined earlier as *Atzmut*. And there is the *Or Ein Sof*, that is, His revelation of Himself. Just as He is infinite, so is His revelation of Himself, the *Or Ein Sof*, infinite. However, God then "condensed" His light through the ten attributes known as the ten *sefirot, chochmah, binah da'at*, and so forth, as was explained previously. Once the infinite light is revealed through the attributes, then we can refer to God as the Knower, the knowledge, and the knowing, because we are not speaking about God Himself but about the way He reveals Himself in a limited creation—His attributes.

This may be compared to sunlight that shines through different colored windowpanes. Although the light is all the same, when it shines through green glass it appears as if the light is green; through blue glass, it appears as if the light is blue. In other words, concerning the way God is in Himself, before he condenses His revelation of Himself into the *sefirot*, the Maharal is correct. On that level, you cannot define God as "knowledge," or "knowing," or even the "Knower." He does not have any definition or attribute whatsoever. You cannot say God and his knowledge are one. You cannot even say that God "knows" Himself! However, after God condensed His light (i.e., His revelation of Himself) into the attributes, in the *sefirot*, then Maimonides is correct, since the attributes are really only a means through which God reveals and manifests Himself. The attributes are God expressing or revealing Himself in a finite way. The true definition

---

32. Chapter 35.

of infinity is that He has no limit, not even the limit that He has to be only limitless. God has the power of finitude as well. This is revealed in the *sefirot*.[33]

GOD'S FOREKNOWLEDGE AND MAN'S FREE CHOICE

Given all of the above, we may now raise a thorny question, one that Maimonides himself asks:[34] Do we not find a paradox between God's knowledge of the future and man's freedom of choice? We must either say that God knows the future and therefore knows whether a person will be good or evil, or else we must say that He does not know. If we say that God knows that a person will be good, then it is impossible for that person to be otherwise, and he has no free choice. Alternatively, if we say that God knows that he will be good, but it is still possible for him to be evil (thus preserving man's free choice), then we must conclude that God's knowledge is incomplete!

Maimonides continues by saying that the answer to this question is vast and involves a great number of important principles and lofty concepts. And, as explained above, God's knowing is part of His Essence[35] and is therefore beyond man's comprehension, just as His Essence is beyond comprehension, as the Prophet states, "My thoughts are not your thoughts; My ways are not your ways" (Isaiah 55:8).

[It is interesting to note that Maimonides did not answer his question in the same way as other authorities and Sages[36]

---

33. See *Avodat HaKodesh*, Rabbi Meir ibn Gabbai, part 1, chap. 8.
34. *Code, Teshuvah* 5:5; *Guide* 3:20.
35. See *Code, Yesodei HaTorah* 2:9–10; *Guide* 3:20, 21.
36. *Midrash Shmuel* to *Pirkei Avot*, chap. 3, in the name of R' Moshe Almoshnino; also cited in *Tosafot Yom Tov, Avot*, ad loc.

answered it—that just as our knowledge of an event is not its cause, but its effect, thus is the knowledge of the Holy One, blessed is He. Only that in His case, He knows the future, because as far as He is concerned it already exists, since the limitations of time and sequence do not apply to Him. Hence, God's foreknowledge of a person's choice occurs because the person already made his choice, as far as God is concerned. It is possible that Maimonides does not give this answer since it is obvious that God does not know in the same way as we know—"My thoughts are not your thoughts; My ways are not your ways" (Isaiah 55:8), as was explained previously. Only regarding human thought does it make sense to speak of knowledge as the result of the event. God's knowing, however, is part of His Essence—by knowing Himself, He knows everything.[37] This is beyond man's comprehension, just as His Essence is beyond man's comprehension. Accordingly, the question mentioned previously still applies.]

Chasidic philosophy explains[38] that God's knowledge of future events is not a contradiction to man's free choice, because the opposite of free choice is not foreknowledge but coercion. That is, free choice means the ability to choose between alternatives without being forced to choose one of the alternatives. Accordingly, foreknowledge and free choice are not diametrically opposed. For example, if a person says that he knows with absolute certainty that if he throws a stone up into the air tomorrow, it will fall to the ground, no one will claim that the stone falls to the ground because that person predicted it or because he knew that it would happen. In fact, the contrary is true. The stone falls to the earth because God made gravity one of the laws of His creation, and therefore a person can know with certainty that tomorrow, too, the

---

37. *Code, Yesodei HaTorah* 2:9–10; *Guide* 3:20, 21.

38. The following sections are based on *Emunah u'Mada*, Rabbi M. M. Schneersohn, pp. 19–26 (Machon Lubavitch, 5740 [1980]; *Shaarei Emunah*, p. 225ff.

stone will fall to the earth if it is thrown into the air. From this, we see that knowledge of an event is not the cause of the event but rather its result. The same is true of man's choice and God's foreknowledge. Since I will make my choices tomorrow without any coercion, therefore, God's knowing what I will do does not force me to do it. His foreknowledge does not determine the future but merely knows the future. Because He is beyond time and space, it is as if my future actions are in the past. That is, His knowledge of the future is like our knowledge of the past. Just as our knowledge of past events, of history, does not determine those events, so, too, His knowledge of future events does not determine future events.

Of course, exactly how God knows the future as we know the past is difficult to explain. And this is why Maimonides says that the matter is beyond human comprehension. God's knowledge is on an infinite level and therefore cannot be grasped by the finite human mind. This is not merely an elegant way of avoiding an answer. The answer is that since God's knowledge of future events is on a level that we cannot comprehend, and of which we are totally unaware, it does not coerce us to act in any way. Hence, man does indeed have free choice.

KNOWLEDGE AND EXISTENCE

However, we can examine the question Maimonides posed regarding God's foreknowledge and man's free choice and examine his answer from an even deeper perspective. Chasidic texts explain[39] that God's thought and knowledge, which knows all created things, encompasses each and every created being from its beginning to its end and its inside and its very core, all in actual

---

39. *Tanya*, chap. 48; see also *Biurei HaZohar* (*Tzemach Tzedek*), p. 266; Discourses 5672, chap. 58ff.

reality (unlike man's thought, which merely visualizes and imagines an object without encompassing it in *actuality*).

For example, in the case of the orb of this earth, God's knowledge encompasses the entire diameter of the globe of the earth, together with all that is in it, from its surface to its deepest level, all in actual reality—for this knowledge constitutes the vitality of the whole sphere of the Earth and its creation *ex nihilo*. Accordingly, since God's knowledge of any given object has such a profound effect upon it that it creates and enlivens it from moment to moment, we would think that there is no free choice at all. After all, a person cannot choose to be born or even to continue living, if this is against the will of God, as was stated explicitly in the *Mishnah*[40]—"against your will you were created, and against your will you were born; against your will you live; and against your will you die." Where, then, is free choice if we are totally dependent upon God's knowledge and thought to even exist? According to this, it would seem that man is indeed forced to do what God knows he will do, for he cannot do anything other than what God knows he will do and still continue to exist. In addition, how do we explain statements of our Sages, such as "Everything is in the hands of Heaven other than the awe of Heaven?"[41]

This is why Maimonides declares[42] that God's existence is totally incomprehensible.[43] Nevertheless, chasidic philosophy gives two explanations of this:

1. Since His knowledge is part of His Essence, we are talking about knowledge that is totally incomprehensible to man, just as His Essence is totally incomprehensible to man.

---

40. *Avot* 4:22.
41. *Berachot* 33b; *Zohar*, vol. 1, p. 59a.
42. *Guide*, part 1, chap. 57.
43. An inadequate translation of *metzivto bitti metziut nimtzah*.

Accordingly, it does not impinge on our consciousness at all and therefore does not affect our free choice.[44]

2. Since He is totally Omnipotent, it is possible for Him to create and maintain existence by way of His thought, as explained earlier, and yet simultaneously ensure that His foreknowledge will not affect our free choice.[45]

TWO REALITIES

This needs clarification. At the beginning of this chapter, we explained that each and every detail of creation, and whatever events take place within all of creation, are meant to be, and also that each and every detail is an integral part of a God's total plan for all of creation and fulfills the purpose for which it was created—in the words of the verse, "God guides the steps of man." Therefore, how can we claim that man is free to choose whatever he wishes, that he has free choice (to the extent that he is rewarded or punished for his choices)?

[It should be pointed out that regarding the Torah and its commandments, the *mitzvahs*, free choice does not mean that one has an option to fulfill the *mitzvahs* or not, as one wishes, and this is therefore the expression of man's free choice. This view is absolutely incorrect. We see that the Torah obligates the fulfillment of the *mitzvahs* and punishes the person who transgresses. Moreover, throughout the era of the *Sanhedrin* (the Jewish Rabbinical Court that existed in Temple times), punishment was meted out by the Court and was administered by its officers for many types of transgressions. Accordingly, "free choice" does not mean that one has an option to do a *mitzvah*, or not do

---

44. Discourses 5672, chap. 58.
45. See *Biurei HaZohar* (*Tzemach Tzedek*), p. 266.

it—one is obligated by the Torah to do it, without any option in the matter.

Rather, regarding the Torah and *mitzvahs*, free choice means that we are not driven by instinct or nature to fulfill the Torah and the *mitzvahs*. An animal does not have free choice because it is driven purely by instinct and its animal nature. An animal does not make choices because it simply reacts to circumstances. When it is hungry, it looks for food; when it is frightened, it runs away; and so forth. A human being, by contrast, has the choice to act upon circumstances, rather than simply to react to circumstances.]

Chasidic texts explain that there are two types of knowing—the way God perceives everything and the way we perceive things. Both are real, for the latter type of knowing was created by God and is not an illusion. It is not to be assumed that our knowledge of things is imaginary because we are on a lower level of awareness than God. Obviously, our knowing is incomparable to His. Nevertheless, it is still knowing.

Reality, the way God sees it, is that He is doing everything and directing everything. At the same time, in our reality, we are acting independently. As far as we are aware, we are not being led one way or another. We are the ones who are making the choice to do the right thing or stay away from the wrong thing. It is a strenuous process. Because of this strain, discipline, and effort that we expend, we deserve to be rewarded whenever we choose to do right. We, with our own effort, with our own strain, made the choice to do the right thing. This is because God created the world in such a way that we are unaware that everything is from God and that we are guided all the time.

11

THE ROLE OF TORAH AND *MITZVAHS*

We explained earlier that Chasidism teaches that even physical matter is ultimately spiritual, and that in every physical thing, even in the inanimate, there is a "soul," which is the creative force that has created it—a being out of nonbeing—and continuously keeps it from reverting back to its former state of nonexistence. It is this "spark" of Godliness that is the true essence and reality of all things. Chasidism further explains that this spark is released and revealed when physical matter is used for a sublime purpose or deed in accordance with the Will of the Creator, as in the performance of a commandment (*mitzvah*). This is called "disencumbering the sparks" (*birur hanitzotzot*). Furthermore, one of the axioms of chasidic thought is that in the final analysis, God can be "comprehended" better by action (the performance of the *mitzvahs*) than by meditation. In this chapter, we will examine these ideas and some of their ramifications.

THE NATURE OF TORAH AND *MITZVAHS*

The majority of the Ten Commandments, which may be regarded as the synopsis of the entire Torah, are basically simple rules that we could have figured out on our own, had they not been given to us by God.[1] After all, we find that Abraham, Isaac, and Jacob observed the entire Torah even before it was given.[2] And in order to observe the commandments of the Torah, they obviously knew the Torah. All the knowledge contained in the Ten Commandments was known and observed for generations, prior to being given at Mount Sinai.[3] In light of this, one must wonder why it was necessary to give the Torah formally to the Jewish people.

The answer given in Chasidism is that the laws of the Torah prior to Mount Sinai were incomparably different from the laws of Torah given at Mount Sinai. God Himself did not command the Patriarchs to follow the laws of the Torah. Rather, through their meditation and Divine service the Patriarchs realized the truth of the Torah. However, the level of spirituality attainable before the Torah was given was limited to the spiritual capacity and sensitivity of each individual.[4]

The great innovation of Mount Sinai was that spiritual achievement was no longer the private domain of especially holy people—it became accessible to all and sundry, even those of a lesser spiritual stature. Although the commandments that the Patriarchs observed remained the same commandments and actions in outer form, their inner content was absolutely transformed by an infinite infusion of Godliness into them. The Talmud explains that this change came about because God put

---

1. *Eruvin* 100b.
2. *Kiddushin* 82a.
3. Ibid.
4. As explained in commentaries to the verse in Exodus 6:3.

Himself into the commandments.[5] Chasidism explains that herein lies the secret of the very essence of the Torah:[6]

The first word of the First Commandment uttered on Mount Sinai, the word *Anochy* ("I am [the Lord your God]") is an acronym, the Talmud[7] explains. That is, the letters of the word spell out an entire sentence—*Ana nafshi chetavit yehavit*. This phrase may be understood simply to mean, "I Myself gave it [the Torah] to you in writing." However, *chasidus* interprets it as meaning, "I gave Myself in writing." That is, when I uttered the Ten Commandments, I gave you Myself![8] This means that the Torah, in effect, is the Essence of God, as stated explicitly in chasidic writings.[9] And this is what was given to us when He gave us the Torah. The Torah is not a mere "handbook for proper living" or a comprehensive guide for conducting human affairs. It is the Essence of God Himself.

Moreover, the Essence of God is in every part of the Torah equally, whether the subject in the Torah concerns the Oneness of God, or whether it concerns the signs of unclean (nonkosher) animals, or whether it mentions Moses or Pharaoh—God is equally within every part of the Torah.[10]

Because of the revelation at Sinai, we can take a physical object and perform a *mitzvah* with it, thus changing the actual physical object into a holy object. This transformation could not be accomplished through our own power. As holy as Abraham,

---

5. *Shabbat* 105a; *Shemot Rabbah* 33:6; *Tanchuma Terumah* 3; *Likkutei Torah Shelach* 48dff.; *Tanya*, chap. 47.

6. *Likkutei Torah Shelach*, 48dff; *Likkutei Sichot*, vol. 19, *Shoftim* 3; the Lubavitcher Rebbe's *Chiddushim u'Biurim b'Shas*, vol. 2, chap. 23.

7. *Shabbat* 105a.

8. See also *Shemot Rabbah* 33:6; *Tanchuma Terumah* 3; *Tanya*, chap. 47.

9. *Likkutei Torah Shelach* 48dff.

10. Maimonides, *Commentary to the Mishnah, Sanhedrin*, chap. 11, principle 8.

Isaac, and Jacob were, they could not transform the physical world into a holy world because, until the Torah was given, spirituality and physicality were two polar opposites.[11] Spirituality meant that a person had to raise himself above the world, transcending the boundaries and limitations of this world, which merely conceal spirituality and Godliness. Spirituality was purely a soul experience, so that for an object to remain physical, and also to be holy, was impossible. Not even the Patriarchs could accomplish this transformation. Whatever the Patriarchs did through serving God remained between their souls and God. It did not transform the physical world into a vessel of Divine revelation.

However, when the Torah was given on Mount Sinai, we were also given the power to transform the physical world into holiness—even while the world remained a physical world—for the two states, physicality and spirituality, no longer contradicted one another. The reason for this is that God put Himself into the Torah, so that the Torah contains exactly the same power as the words God said at Mount Sinai.

From the foregoing, we can understand why it is essential to the Jewish faith that we believe that the Torah was given by God. Were it merely given by Moses, who was inspired by God, or in any other way, the Torah would not have the power to transform the physical into spiritual and nevertheless remain a physical, time-and-space-bound object.[12]

---

11. As in the verse in Psalms 115:16: "The Heavens are God's, and the earth He gave to Man." This was prior to the giving of the Torah, as was stated in *Shemot Rabbah* 12:3.

12. Regarding the above, see *Likkutei Torah, Bamidbar*, 15cff; *Likkutei Sichot*, vol. 8, p. 21ff.

SANCTIFYING THE PHYSICAL WORLD

The Midrash[13] poses a troublesome question: Since the Torah
was given to us to teach us the commandments, why does it begin
with the story of Genesis, rather than with the first commandment of the Torah, the mitzvah to sanctify the month at the earliest
sighting of the new moon?[14] The Midrash answers that by
beginning the Torah with the story of creation, God declared the
power of His deeds to His people. The nations of the world
complain that the Jewish people are thieves, for they conquered
the land of seven nations (Israel) and kept it for themselves. God
therefore declares that the entire earth belongs to Him, for He
created it, and He may give it to whomever He pleases. He saw fit
to give the Jewish people the land of Israel.

Kabbalistic[15] and chasidic[16] works offer a fascinating explanation of this midrashic source:

"You have conquered the land of the seven nations" means, in
a spiritual sense, that the Jewish people have sanctified the
mundane things of this world by using them for holy purposes—
the fulfillment of the Torah and mitzvahs. In this way, they have
transferred them from the realm of the merely permissible to the
restricted realm of holiness, from which the nations of the world
are, by and large, excluded.

The complaint of the nations of the world is thus "you are
thieves, for you have conquered the land of the seven nations"—
that is, those things that were previously under the jurisdiction of
the mundane, to which the nations of the world are connected, by
bringing them into the realm of holiness from which they are
generally restricted.

---

13. See Bereishit Rabbah 1:2; Rashi, Genesis 1:1.
14. See Exodus 12:2.
15. Emek HaMelech, Rabbi Naphtali Bachrach, beginning.
16. Or HaTorah (Tzemach Tzedek), Bo, p. 262; Likkutei Sichot, vol. 20,
p. 2ff.

Elsewhere the *Midrash*[17] compares this to Jacob and Esau, who divided the worlds between them, Esau claiming this world, and Jacob the World to Come. Consequently, when the descendants of Jacob (the Jewish people) "conquer" the mundane by broadening the realm of holiness,[18] the nations of the world regard this as theft—for it formerly belonged to the realm of the mundane.

The Jewish people nevertheless have an answer to this complaint: "The entire earth belongs to God, for He created it, and He may give it to whomever He pleases." The fact that prior to the Divine service of a Jew, the realm of the mundane "belonged" to the nations of the world was only because He originally gave it to them as a result of the Sin of the Tree of Knowledge of Good and Evil. However, this was not His ultimate intention. The ultimate purpose of creation is to "make a dwelling for God in this world"—that is, to broaden the realm of holiness, so that it encompasses everything that it encompassed prior to the Sin of the Tree of Knowledge. This is the rectification of that sin.

This, then, is the kabbalistic and chasidic explanation of why the Torah should have begun with the *mitzvah* of the sanctification of the new month, rather than with the story of Genesis, for the Torah is superior to creation[19] and also superior to the work of conquering creation and sublimating it to holiness.

However, the Torah actually begins with the account of creation, for even though the work of conquering the physical world and sublimating it to the realm of holiness is on a lower level than Torah and *mitzvahs, per se*, nevertheless, the purpose of creation—"to make a dwelling place for the Holy One, blessed is He, in the lower worlds"—is fulfilled to a greater extent by sublimating the world than by the fulfillment of Torah and

---

17. *Seder Eliyahu Zuta*, chap. 19; *Yalkut Shimoni, Toldot*, para. 111.

18. See *Emek HaMelech*, op cit.; *Me'or Einayim* (Rabbi Nachum of Tchernobyl), *Toldot*, cited in *Or HaTorah*, loc cit., vol. 4, p. 799bff.

19. See *Or HaTorah*, ibid.

mitzvahs, per se. And the reason for this is that it penetrates even the realm of the merely permissible, whereas Torah and *mitzvahs* never leave the restricted realm of holiness.[20]

Correspondingly, regarding man himself, the work of elevating and sublimating this world—extracting and refining the sparks from the shattered vessels of the world of *tohu*—demands that he draw upon the powers of his soul in a far deeper way than if he remained constantly immersed in the realm of holiness, as will be discussed later.

THE ULTIMATE SACRIFICE

This can be better understood by examining an incident recorded in the Torah[21] regarding two of the sons of Aaron, the High Priest. Shortly after the Tabernacle was erected, Nadav and Avihu each took a censer, filled it with glowing coals, and made an incense offering to God, which they had not been commanded to do. Both of them were killed instantly by a fire "which went out from before the Lord."

The reason for their punishment by death is not stated explicitly in the verse, but the *Midrash* offers several possible explanations: They entered the holiest area of the Tabernacle, the Holy of Holies, without permission;[22] they were not wearing the required dress when serving in the Tabernacle;[23] neither of them had children;[24] or they were not married.[25]

Furthermore, it is not understood how Nadav and Avihu could

---

20. See also *Likkutei Sichot*, vol. 15, p. 245.

21. Leviticus 10:1–5, 16:1.

22. *Torat Kohanim, Acharei,* beg.; *Vayikrah Rabbah* 20:8; *Bamidbar Rabbah* 2:23.

23. *Vayikrah Rabbah* 20:9; *Tanchuma, Acharei,* beg.

24. *Vayikrah Rabbah* 20:9; *Tanchuma, Acharei,* beg.

25. Ibid.

have sinned in the first place. The Sages explain[26] that after their deaths, Moses commentated to Aaron: "My brother, I knew that the Tabernacle would be consecrated through those who know God and are beloved to Him. I thought that it would be through you or I, but now I see that they [Nadav and Avihu] are greater than you or me!"

Chasidic texts[27] explain that the "sin" of Aaron's sons was not a sin in the normal sense of the word, but the result of a tremendously powerful desire to cleave to the Holy One, blessed is He, which brought them to a state of ecstasy in which their souls literally expired. This is what the verse states: ". . . after the death of the two sons of Aaron when they drew near God and died" (Leviticus 16:1). Their drawing near to God is regarded as a sin, for even though a person must aspire to come close to God, to the extent that his soul even leaves his body,[28] nevertheless, at the same time, even when in the state of "expiration of soul," a person must arouse within himself the willingness and desire to return to the service required by a soul within a body in this world. In other words, to adhere to the demand to make a dwelling place for God precisely in the material world below. The intention is not to fade blissfully into the spiritual realm of nonbeing, but to live in the world and make the world itself a fit receptacle for the Holy One, blessed is He. Since Nadav and Avihu did not have this intention, their expiration of soul was regarded as a sin.

Each of the opinions regarding their transgression reflects the same central theme—expiration of soul without the desire to live in

---

26. Rashi, Leviticus 10:3 from *Torat Kohanim, Shemini*; Talmud, *Zevachim* 115b.

27. In the discourses entitled *Acharei Mot* 5649; *Acharei Mot* 11, Nissan 5722; *Likkutei Sichot* (Hebrew version), vol. 3, p. 248ff. See also the commentary of *Or HaChaim* on the verse.

28. See *Shulchan Aruch HaRav, Orach Chaim*, chap. 98; ibid, *Yoreh De'ah, Hilchot Talmud Torah* 4:5.

this world and make it a dwelling place for God. "They entered the Holy of Holies without permission"—their souls soared aloft, to the very highest of levels, and they ignored the mission of making a vessel for Godliness out of this world. "They were not wearing the required dress"—garments signify the practical commandments[29] that are fulfilled, using the stuff of this world. They aspired to cleave to the purely spiritual while ignoring the material world, not realizing that God can be "comprehended" better by the performance of the *mitzvahs* than by meditation and expiration of the soul. "Neither of them were married, or they had no children," contrary to the requirement of making the world a settled, orderly place "He did not create it [for the sake of] chaos, but to be settled."[30]

Of course, this does not mean in any way that meditation is anathema to the Jewish spirit. The opposite is true. However, entering the most sacrosanct realms through deep meditation must be tempered by the intention to bring Divine revelation into the world. Moreover, this intention must exist prior to the process of spiritual ascent.[31]

An incident recorded in the Talmud[32] illustrates this concept further: Four talmudic Sages of very high repute, Ben Azzai, Ben Zoma, Rabbi Akiva, and Acher,[33] entered the *Pardess* (literally, "orchard," a euphemism for the highest levels of spiritual ecstasy). Prior to their entering this level, Rabbi Akiva warned the other Sages, "When you come to the place of pure marble stones, do not say, 'water, water.'"[34] In other words, Rabbi Akiva told them that at that level, it is forbidden to suggest separation or division of

---

29. See *Tanya*, chap. 5; *Iggeret HaKodesh* (*Tanya*, part 4), chap. 29.

30. Isaiah 45:18.

31. *Likkutei Sichot*, vol. 3, p. 250.

32. *Chagiga* 14b.

33. Literally, "the other one." His real name, Elisha ben Avuya, is not mentioned, in accordance with the prayer that the name of the wicked be forgotten.

34. *Chagiga* 14b.

any sort, "water, water" (indicating that there are two levels or types of water, the essential for life in this world), for at that level there is only absolute unity.[35]

Of all the Sages who entered this level, only Rabbi Akiva returned safe and sound. Acher became a heretic, Ben Zoma lost his mind, and Ben Azzai "perceived and died." According to talmudic sources,[36] he, too, was unmarried and did not have children. Chasidus explains that this was because he had no desire to return to the world.[37] The same is true of Ben Zoma.[38]

Rabbi Akiva, however, "returned in peace" because he had originally "entered in peace." His intention from the outset was to fulfill the Supernal Will and infuse the world with Godliness.[39]

The ultimate self-sacrifice, then, is to live properly in the world, not to leave it. One does not have to live in a monastery or an ashram, or become a hermit in order to be holy. On the contrary, true holiness means living in the world, while at the same time transcending the world.

NOTHING FOR NOTHING

The "interface" of Torah and *mitzvahs* and Divine providence with the purpose of man on this earth can be best understood[40] by examining a chasidic understanding of the talmudic dictum "Of everything which the Holy One, blessed is He, created in His world, He created nothing without a purpose."[41]

---

35. *Arizal*, cited in *Or HaTorah Beshallach*, p. 480.

36. *Sotah* 4b.

37. *Likkutei Sichot*, vol. 3, p. 250.

38. See *Bereishit Rabbah* 2:4.

39. See, further, *Likkutei Sichot*, vol. 3, p. 251, n. 14.

40. For the following analysis, see *Reshimot* of the Lubavitcher Rebbe, Rabbi M. M. Schneerson, Issue 44 (*Bamidbar*), 1996.

41. *Shabbat* 77b.

Midrashic sources[42] explain the purpose and benefit of the creation of a spider, for example: When David was trying to escape the wrath of Saul, he hid in a cave. The Holy One, blessed is He, sent a spider to weave a web over the mouth of the cave, so that when King Saul came upon the cave in his search for the elusive David, he did not bother to search there, since no one could have bypassed the spider's web in order to hide in the recesses of the cave.

This principle applies not only to each and every created entity, but also to each and every event in the universe—there is no event that is random or purposeless. Everything is by Divine intervention—*hashgacha pratit*—which also applies to the inanimate, plant, and animal realms, as in the famous statement of the Ba'al Shem Tov,[43] regarding a leaf or a straw blowing in the wind—that this, too, is by Divine providence and fulfills a special purpose, as was explained previously. The Alter Rebbe, Rabbi Shneur Zalman of Liadi, adduced a proof for this from a statement of one of the Sages of the Talmud:[44] When Rabbi Yochanan saw a heron swooping down to catch a fish, he said, "Your judgments are [in] the great deep," (Psalms 36:7), for "you sent a heron to carry out your judgment upon the fish of the sea, and kill those whose time has come to die" (Rashi).

It is obvious that this applies to human beings, and everything that happens to them, for "a person does not bang his finger . . . unless this is decreed from above."[45] Similarly, if a person puts his hand into his pocket to take out three coins, and at first he manages to fish out only two, this is in order to cause him "suffering out of love."[46] Also, "a person's legs lead him to the place where it has been decreed that he go,"[47] and so on.

---

42. Cf. *Otzar Midrashim*, vol. 1 (Eizenshtein), p. 74. See also *Targum Yonatan, Tehillim* 57:3.

43. See *Kesser Shem Tov*, additions, para. 119ff.

44. *Chullin* 63a.

45. *Chullin* 7b.

46. *Arachin* 16b.

47. *Sukkah* 53a.

This is the rule: There is no thing, matter, or deed that is without a purpose.

Man and the world were created because "the Holy One, blessed is He, desired a dwelling place in the lower worlds,"[48] which is achieved through the mitzvahs that man fulfills, utilizing the things of this world. In this regard our Sages state, "All of them were not created other than to serve me [man], and I was not created other than to serve my Master."[49]

Accordingly, all of man's deeds, and everything that happens to him, is all so that he can fulfill that which he was commanded to do—to serve his Master. This applies whether he serves his Master by way of the deed or event itself, or whether the deed or event is only a means toward the goal of serving his Master. There is no thing or event that is excluded from this rule, for everything that the Holy One, blessed is He, created in his world may be divided into three categories: that which is forbidden; that which is a mitzvah; and that which is permissible.

Regarding the categories of that which is forbidden and that which is a *mitzvah*, a person is obligated to use the things in the category of *mitzvahs* to perform *mitzvahs*, and to reject those which are in the category of the forbidden.[50] Regarding the category of those things that are permissible—these must be transformed by man into the category of *mitzvahs*. This is possible through "knowing Him in all your ways,"[51] and doing "all of your deeds for the sake of Heaven."[52]

Accordingly, at every moment of a person's life and in whatever situation he finds himself, of all the possible acts that he can do ("all of your deeds") in the next moment, and of all the possible ways in which he could go ("in all your ways") in the moment following the present one, only one way and one deed will be the

---

48. *Tanchuma, Nasso* 16; *Tanya*, chap. 36.

49. *Kiddushin*, end.

50. In this way, he fulfills a positive commandment or avoids transgressing a prohibition.

51. *Mishlei* 3:6.

52. *Avot* 2:12.

proper one—the way or deed that will lead to the fulfillment of that which he has been commanded (guarding himself from that which is forbidden, fulfilling the *mitzvahs*, and transforming the permissible into *mitzvahs*).

Besides this, there is no other possibility, for if he did not do precisely the necessary thing at that point in time, then:

Either he committed a transgression (regarding that which is forbidden);

Or, he failed to fulfill a *mitzvah* (regarding that which is a *mitzvah*), which is also a transgression;

Or, he did not fulfill a *hiddur mitzvah* (he did not do the *mitzvah* in the best possible way), according to the principle of, "this is my Lord and I will glorify Him."[53] If a person is able to do a *hiddur mitzvah* and did not do so, this is also regarded as a transgression;

Or, he did not transform the permissible into a *mitzvah*, by not acting for the sake of Heaven. Even where there is a need of the body, or its very preservation and life, but his intention is not for the sake of Heaven . . . it flows and is drawn from the second level of *kelipos* and *sitra achra*[54] . . . [*kelipat nogah*][55] . . . and a trace of it remains in the body. Therefore, the body must undergo the Purgatory of the Grave (*chibut hakever*) . . . to cleanse and purge it of its [spiritual] impurity.[56]

Accordingly, when a person hears or sees something, or he gains additional insight into something, and so on, this is (1) not for nothing. Rather, out of all the possibilities that exist with regard to the ultimate purpose and aim of the thing or event, (2) there is only one way before him regarding that which must be done immediately afterwards, and (3) thereby fulfill the commandment and obligation incumbent upon him—by doing a *mitzvah*.

---

53. *Numbers* 15:2, *Shabbat* 133b.

54. Terms denoting unholiness and evil.

55. *Kelipat Nogah* is an intermediate category between holiness and evil. Sometimes this level is absorbed and elevated to the category of holiness, as when the good within it is extracted from the bad, and it prevails and ascends until it is absorbed in holiness.

56. *Tanya*, chaps. 7, 8.

The same principle applies to every matter, object, and deed in this world and in all of the worlds.

For example: If a person learned, let's say, about the world of Atzilut,[57] either he fulfilled a mitzvah through the very study itself, or this will bring him to fulfill a mitzvah—as, for example, in his prayer (because it will help his meditation before praying, and his concentration during his prayers), and so on. Moreover, it is only for this reason that he came to know about the world of Atzilut, so that this knowledge will be used for a mitzvah.

Had it not been possible (and thus there would have been no obligation) that this specific thing or event would lead to a mitzvah, this thing or event would not have been part of the person's life or experience, since the entire purpose of its creation is so that this person can use it for a mitzvah. Accordingly, the two other possible explanations for the presence of the object or the occurrence of the event—that it is by chance, or that it is by Divine Providence (hashgacha pratit) but that it does not fulfill any particular purpose in the fulfillment of a mitzvah—are invalidated. One must say that the event took place, or the thing exists, only in order to enable a person to do a mitzvah, for there is nothing that exists for any other purpose. . . .

Another example is given by Rabbi Shneur Zalman of Liadi:

One who eats fat beef [generally frowned upon by the Rabbis after the destruction of the Temple] and drinks spiced wine in order to broaden his mind for the service of God and His Torah; as Ravah said, "Wine and fragrance [make a man's mind more receptive],"[58] or in order to fulfill the command concerning enjoyment of the Sabbath and Festivals.[59] In such a case the vitality of the meat and

---

57. A highly elevated, spiritual plane of existence.

58. *Yoma* 76a.

59. *Maimonides, Code, Shabbat* 30:7; *Shulchan Aruch HaRav* 242:1, 529:1–529: 3.

wine, originating in the *kelipat nogah*, is distilled and ascend to God like a burnt offering and sacrifice.[60]

Note that celibacy, in and of itself, is not the purpose. Rather, the idea is that the permissible realm of this world can be elevated by "knowing Him in all your ways,"[61] and doing "all of your deeds for the sake of Heaven," and thus fulfilling the injunction to make a dwelling place for God in this world. If one cannot do this, for whatever reason, then that aspect of the permissible is to be avoided by that person, although not necessarily by another.

---

60. *Tanya*, chap. 7.
61. Proverbs 3:6.

3
DIVINE SERVICE

12

Eliciting God's Essence

The previous sections have concentrated primarily on chasidic ontological and cosmological views, with only a glimpse of their implementation in a person's daily life, as seen from the chasidic viewpoint. In Jewish life in general, and in Chasidism in particular, theory and practice must be completely integrated. The glib Aristotelian philosophy of "this is Aristotle, the philosopher [who spoke about the perfection of man and how his intellect must rule over his passions], and this is Aristotle, the man" (who was caught in an embarrassing situation with one of his students) is absolutely anathema to Jewish thinking—"anyone whose outside is not like his inside may not enter the house of study,"[1] in the words of one of the great tannaitic Sages. Put another way, the question we must ask is how chasidic philosophy harmonizes the divine plan for creation with the duty of man in this world.

At the beginning of this essay, it was mentioned that according

---

1. *Berachot* 28a. See also *Zohar,* vol. 3, pp. 230a, 235b, 245b.

to chasidic philosophy, God can be "comprehended" better by action (the performance of the *mitzvahs*) than by meditation.[2] In the remainder of this chapter, we will explain the meaning and import of this statement.

In a large number of chasidic discourses, we find that the emphasis is on action—"the main thing is the deed."[3] The purpose of the descent of the soul into the body, and the purpose of the entire creation, declare these discourses, is the performance of the *mitzvahs*—that is, the fulfillment of the commandments set out in the Torah (see, e.g., Tanya, chaps. 35–37). In contrast, intellectual comprehension and the arousal of the emotions are not regarded as an end in themselves, but as secondary. Their purpose is to vitalize the fulfillment of the *mitzvahs*. In the terms used previously, comprehension and emotion elicit "only" *Or Ein Sof*, "revelation"—whereas the *mitzvahs* grasp *Atzmut*, "the essence of God."

Paradoxically, however, we find in an equally large number of chasidic discourses that God wants the "heart"[4] no less than He wants the actual fulfillment of the *mitzvahs*. According to chasidic texts,[5] the Torah and *mitzvahs* that a person fulfills without love and awe are unable to ascend above and remain stagnant and lifeless in this world. Moreover, when these aspects are missing in the fulfillment of the *mitzvahs*, even though the activity has been performed perfectly in every other respect, the *mitzvah* is regarded as missing its ultimate purpose, for "the *mitzvahs* were given only to purify man."[6] This purification comes about as a result of a person's self-subjugation, fulfilling the will of God even though it

---

2. In the entire following chapter, I have been greatly helped by an essay written by Rabbi Yoel Kahan, part of which has been published in *Be'er HaChassidus—Ohalei Lubavitch*, p. 87ff.

3. *Avot* 1:17.

4. *Sanhedrin* 106b.

5. See *Tanya*, p. 53b.

6. *Bereishit Rabbah*, chap. 44.

may be against his own will—"Fulfill His will as you would your own will . . . set aside your will because of His will."[7]

Thus, on the one hand, "the actual deed is the main thing," even if it is devoid of feeling and mystical intention (*kavvanah*),[8] for it is precisely the *mitzvahs* that draw down *Atzmut*. True, a *mitzvah* performed without love and awe, and without *kavvanah*, draws down *Atzmut* in such a way that it remains concealed; but since "hidden" and "concealed" are terms that do not even apply to *Atzmut*, why the demand for intention and emotional arousal? What difference do they make to God's *Atzmut*? Granted, that in terms of man, purification of his soul and his feelings comes about explicitly through love and awe of God and his subjugation to God, but again, what difference does that make to God? Since the goal has been achieved—Godliness has been drawn into the world by the practical performance of the *mitzvahs*—what difference does it make whether the individual is purified thereby or not?

On the other hand, in chapter 6 we explained that although the actual performance of the *mitzvahs* connects the world with *Atzmut*, this connection is not revealed unless the *mitzvahs* are fulfilled with love and awe.[9] In terms of the analogy used there—although the performance of the *mitzvahs* makes a home for God in this world, nevertheless, the illumination of His home is though their fulfillment with love and awe.[10] Furthermore, if the *mitzvah* was done for the wrong reasons (*shelo lishmah*), not only is God not revealed, His presence is actually obscured.[11]

In *Tanya* (chaps. 35–37), Rabbi Shneur Zalman explains that the soul is not the primary beneficiary of the fulfillment of the

---

7. *Avot* 2:4.
8. See *Tanya*, chap. 38.
9. Ibid., para. 5.
10. See *Tanya*, chap. 38, at length.
11. See *Likkutei Sichot*, p. 1054.

mitzvahs, which are performed using the material objects of this world. On the contrary, Torah study and meditation draw down *Or Ein Sof* upon the soul to a far greater degree than the performance of the practical *mitzvahs*. Rather, the main beneficiaries of the *mitzvahs* are the world (which is made into a "home" for the Holy One), the person's body that performs the *mitzvah* (such as the arm around which the phylacteries are wrapped), and the animal soul.[12]

The major corollary of this is that man's task in the world, and the ultimate purpose of his creation, is not for his own benefit, so that he can achieve spiritual purification and perfection. Rather, his function is to make the world a home for God's *Atzmut*, and by doing so, he fulfills the purpose of the descent of his soul. In fact, "the [Godly][13] soul itself does not require rectification,"[14] for it is inherently "part of God above"[15] True, one of the thirteen principles of Judaism is that a person is ultimately rewarded for his performance of the *mitzvahs*.[16] Nevertheless, a *chasid* is one who seeks the welfare of his fellow, even if this may not be in his own interest,[17] to the extent that "a *chasid* is one who relinquishes his own certain benefit in order to do a favor for another, even if there is some doubt that he will succeed in his attempt to do a favor for another."[18]

It is obvious that by devoting oneself to the welfare of others and by dedicating oneself to fulfilling the demands of "making a home in the lower world," one achieves the highest level that a

---

12. See Chapter 4 of this book.
13. As opposed to the animal soul.
14. *Tanya*, chaps. 37, 38.
15. *Tanya*, chap. 2.
16. See the eleventh of Maimonides' Thirteen Principles.
17. This is the definition of a *Hasid* given by the Sages in *Berachot*. See also chap. 4 of this book.
18. *Likkutei Sichot*, vol. 3, p. 800, citing *Sefer HaSichot 5700*, pp. 32, 33.

human being is capable of achieving, because relinquishing all of one's personal benefit, even the spiritual delight of cleaving to God, for the sake of fulfilling God's desire for a home in the lower worlds, is the highest level of self-nullification, or better, self-transcendence.

Nevertheless, it must be noted that Chasidism does not stress awareness of the greatness of *mitzvahs* and the nobility of seeking out the welfare of others. On the contrary, the emphasis is on the importance of the act itself—in other words, that the world becomes a dwelling place for God—and not on the emotional or spiritual high or the infinite reward that will surely ensue[19] as a result of his doing this.

BITTUL

This highlights one of the fundamental teachings of Chasidism—that holiness (i.e., the alighting of Godliness upon something) is directly proportional to the recipient's level of *bittul* (self-nullification, or self-transcendence).[20]

The *bittul* experienced by a person through the actual fulfillment of the *mitzvahs* (and, consequently, the revelation of Godliness—his reward—proportional to his level of *bittul*) is much greater than the *bittul* that brought him to actually fulfill the *mitzvah*. The reason for this is that the *bittul* and the concomitant revelation granted to a person by God cannot be achieved by man alone through his own efforts—this can only be achieved by a person through the Supernal Will that is elicited through his fulfillment of the *mitzvahs*.[21]

---

19. *Likkutei Torah*, *Re'eh*, p. 28d.
20. See *Tanya*, chap. 35, and, particularly, the note on p. 44b.
21. See *Tanya*, chaps. 23, 52.

Moreover, just as a person cannot directly achieve this *bittul* and revelation through his own efforts (but only by means of the *mitzvahs*), so, too, he cannot detract from the results of the performance of a *mitzvah*. The classical examples of this are: If a Jew was forced by gentiles to eat *matzah* on Passover (one of the positive commandments), even though he resisted vigorously, he has fulfilled the *mitzvah*. Similarly, Maimonides rules[22] that it is permitted for the Rabbinical Court to force a man to give his wife a bill of divorce (where the circumstances require), and the divorce is entirely valid, even though normally a divorce given unwillingly is invalid. Since God's will has been fulfilled (by the observance of a *mitzvah*) even if the person himself is opposed to doing the *mitzvah*, and even if he never intended to do it, nevertheless the Divine will has been fulfilled and "the light and life of the Supreme Will issue forth to be clothed in the worlds."[23]

BITTUL OF THE SOUL AND THE BODY

Chasidic texts[24] point out that the level of *bittul* achieved by the soul through making a home for God down here in this world is far superior to the natural *bittul* that is an inherent aspect of the soul by virtue of it being a descendent of the Patriarchs.[25]

The soul itself is "truly part of God Above."[26] In other words, the soul is inherently Divine. As such, its self-nullification before God is not something the person has to acquire through his own

---

22. *Code, Geirushin.*

23. *Tanya*, chap. 23.

24. Explained in *Tze'ena u'Re'ena 5650*, and the discourses of: *12th of Tammuz 5697*; *Shavuot 5706*; *Kadosh Yisrael 5718*; *Sefer Ha'Arachim*, s.v. *Ahava*—addenda.

25. See *Tanya*, chap. 18ff.

26. *Tanya*, chap. 2, citing a verse in Job 31:2.

efforts; it is an essential trait of the Jewish soul. Accordingly, this level of *bittul* is not self-transcending—in the sense of subjugating itself to the will of the Creator, even when His will opposes your will. On the contrary, the natural tendency of the soul is to willingly cleave to God (*deveikut*).[27] In contrast, when a worldly object, such as a pair of phylacteries made of animal hide, is wound around the arm and the head in fulfillment of the precept of *tefillin*, or even when the human body is made to submit itself to God—"willingly, and in the case of the true mystic, even eagerly"[28]—this level of *bittul* directly opposes its existence, which is to be "something," rather than "nothing." Thus, when this happens, the *bittul* achieved is total.

This requires further explanation: When the soul submits itself to God, this does not give full expression to God's unity ("there is nothing besides Him") for the natural state of the soul is to cleave to God and merge with its Source. However, when a worldly object submits itself to God, there is no admixture of any element in this *bittul* other than God—that is, the *bittul* experienced by the material world is not a result of its inherent nature. On the contrary—its inherent nature is to fell itself as an existence that is totally unaware of its source. It is only because of God's true unity—"there is nothing besides Him"—that created beings of the material world are also completely nullified.

When a soul clothed in a physical body in this world fulfills its mission of making a home for God in the lower worlds, thus bringing about a true level of *bittul*—submission by fulfilling the *mitzvahs*—then the soul also achieves this self-transcending level of *bittul*.

Since this level of *bittul*—the highest level possible—comes

---

27. *Tanya*, chap. 35.

28. See the Lubavitcher Rebbe's letter written to the organizers of the International Seminar on Jewish Mysticism, with which we began this study.

about by way of the actual performance of the *mitzvahs*, a person's *kavvanah* in fulfilling the *mitzvahs* must be "without the intent of receiving reward."[29] A person's intention should therefore be, "I was created for nothing other than to serve my Maker."[30] Thus, a person, not feeling his own existence in the serving of his Maker, achieves the highest level of *bittul*.

In this way, the true Oneness of God is expressed—in other words, the Oneness of *Atzmut*. For when a material object that feels itself to be an entity independent of its source and that feels as if its existence is of its essence, to the extent that it can proclaim (as Pharaoh did), "The river is mine, and I made myself"[31]— when such a material object submits itself willingly to God, this the very highest level of *bittul*: "Attachment to God out of free choice is far greater than attachment to Him out of necessity."[32] The oneness of the *Or Ein Sof*, however, is akin to the natural *bittul* of the soul—it is one only "because it is like the luminary," but not because it has submitted itself to its Source.

As we pointed out earlier, chasidic philosophy emphasizes that His existence is of His Essence, and that consequently, He is the only "true" existence—that is, the only existence that is totally independent of any other existence, and all the rest of existence is dependent upon His existence.[33] Thus, His existence is called "necessary existence." His existence cannot be observed or delimited so that we can say what He is.[34] Rather, His existence negates all positive descriptions and all negative descriptions,[35] and He is only that He is whatever He truly is, and therefore He

---

29. See *Avot* 1:3.

30. *Kiddushin*, end.

31. Ezekiel 29:3.

32. *Likkutei Sichot*, vol. 4, p. 1341, and n. 14.

33. *Derech Mitzevotecha*, pp. 46b, 57a; *Sefer HaMa'amarim 5666*, p. 169; *Sefer HaMa'amarim 5677*, pp. 72–73.

34. See Maimonides' *Moreh Nevuchin*, pt. 1, chap. 57.

35. *Vayolech Hashem, Ma'amarim 5666*.

is absolutely One. This oneness is fully expressed in the willing submission of a person to his Creator through the fulfillment of His Supernal Will clothed in the *mitzvahs*.

Paradoxically, then, this level of absolute unity, the Oneness of *Atzmut*, cannot be revealed to the soul within itself, just as it cannot be revealed in the *Or Ein Sof*. It can only be revealed through the creation (for only *Atzmut* can create) and through the physical body, the vehicle through which the soul performs the Divinely ordained *mitzvahs*—these make a home for God in the lowest of worlds. The "spark" of Godliness that is the true Essence and reality of all things is released and revealed when physical objects are used by the physical body in fulfilling the Will of the Creator by performing a commandment (*mitzvah*). Accordingly, it follows that the performance of the *mitzvahs* is of utmost importance in chasidic philosophy. The fear of antinomianism is therefore certainly unjustified, as history has, in fact, proved— *Chasidim* have become the bastion and symbol of religious adherence. In the final analysis, the mystical message of Chasidism is that God's *Atzmut* can be "comprehended" better by action (the performance of the *mitzvahs*) than by meditation. This revelation is indeed a mystical revolution.

INDEX

About the Author

Noson Gurary is an ordained rabbi and Jewish judge. He received his rabbinical ordination at the United Lubavitcher Yeshiva in Brooklyn, New York. He recently received his doctorate in Jewish philosophy from the Moscow Lomonosov University in Russia. Rabbi Gurary is currently the executive director of the *Chabad* Houses in upstate New York and has taught in the Judaic Studies Department at State University of New York, Buffalo, for the past twenty-four years. He is the author of *The Thirteen Principles of Faith: A Chasidic Viewpoint,* has published numerous articles in rabbinical publications, and has lectured on campuses all over the United States. Rabbi Gurary lives in Buffalo, New York, with his wife and seven children.